The California Trail Yesterday & Today

To those who've gone before

To those met along the way

and to those yet to follow

The California Trail Yesterday & Today

A Pictorial Journey Along the California Trail

By
William E. Hill

PRUETT **P** PUBLISHING COMPANY
Boulder, Colorado

First Edition

1 2 3 4 5 6 7 8 9

Printed in the United States of America

Library of Congress Cataloging-in-Publication Data

Hill, William E.
    The California Trail.

    Bibliography: p.
    Includes index.
    1. California Trail—History. 2. California Trail— History—Pictorial works. 3. West (U.S.)—Description and travel—1848-1860. 4. West (U.S.)—Description and travel—1848-1860—Views. 5. Overland journeys to the Pacific. 6. Overland journeys to the Pacific—Pictorial works. 7. West (U.S.)—Description and travel—1981-   —Guide-books. I. Title.
F593.H55   1986   978   86-91527
ISBN0-87108-712-X

Contents

Acknowledgments vi

Foreword vii

California-Oregon Trail Map........................ viii-ix

Title Song: "Sweet Betsy from Pike"................ x

Preface 1

Early History of the California Trail 8

Maps-Guides-Diaries-Artists 21

Guidebooks 33

Diaries... 40

Artists 60

Pictorial Journey 62

Museums and Displays 172

Additional Reading 179

Bibliography 182

Index 186

Acknowledgments

As with any work many people have helped by providing encouraging words, critical reviews, directions and information on the trail, and cooperation at various libraries and historical societies. While many could easily be noted, thanks must be given to those special few who most deserve it because they best represent those who assisted.

Over the years many ranchers were encountered, and almost all allowed me to walk around and drive through their places. Many, like the Stevensons and the Bucks, however, took not just minutes, but hours and parts of working days to talk about the local history, the trail, its location, artifacts found, and anything they thought might be either interesting or helpful.

While some libraries and photographic divisions need better coordination, most libraries and historical societies were very cooperative. Linda Wickert, the Fine Arts Curator at the California Historical Society was very cooperative and went the "extra mile" when she easily could have done otherwise.

Many park superintendents, such as Wayne Brandt at Rock Creek and Jerry Banta at Scotts Bluff, should be singled out for their pride in their work and cooperation when providing access and information.

Certain individuals on a personal level gave me that extra spark. Helen Henderson's simple but encouraging words of "Do it!" when I was hesitant and first thinking about writing about the emigrant trails provided the boost I needed to get started. My parents, brothers, and sisters constant inquiries about my progress kept me going. And my father and son who at times were my partner while driving along on many of the desolate regions of the trails provided someone to try ideas out on and to provide help as needed.

Foreword

The California gold rush was an epic event, a sudden and irradiating explosion of energy by the American people. Before 1849 the bold democratic experiment—something unique in the annals of mankind—had been largely confined to lands east of the Mississippi River; the lands west thereof were generally understood to be hostile and uninhabitable. Acquisition of California, after the war with Mexico, caused no stampede. What caused it was the electrifying news of gold at Sutter's Mill, and the resultant gold fever that afflicted over two million Americans.

To reach distant California roughly half of these adventurers went by sea, either around Cape Horn or via land links across Panama or Mexico. The other half traveled by land. There was just one land route that had the virtue of being centrally located and heading straight west—the great Platte River Road that led to South Pass, providential gateway through the Rocky Mountain barrier. While the seafarers also helped to populate California, the overland emigrants with their ox- or mule-powered covered wagons performed the additional feat of breaking the wilderness barrier, thus making possible the transformation of the United States into a truly transcontinental Union.

William Hill's book is about these landlubber Argonauts and their incredible two thousand mile journey from jumping-off points along the Missouri River, across the dangerous wilderness of prairies, plains, deserts, and mountains to their ultimate destination, California. His book is designed for casual readers who may be content with a bird's-eye view of the overland experience, with samplings from the rich source materials. He has his facts commendably straight, and recommends other authoritative books for those inspired to explore the subject in greater depth. Of exceptional interest are selected contemporary maps and the illustrations of three rare and gifted trail artists. The author himself supplies excellent photographs of trail scenes today, taken on field trips to retrace the route to California and relive in imagination the golden odyssey of the Forty-niners.

The California Trail Yesterday and Today is a timely and welcome addition to a rapidly growing body of literature, both popular and scholarly, on a subject of perennial fascination. For all our revolutionary technical advances that compress time and space—so that we might, for example, travel from Missouri to California in three hours instead of the several months it took in 1849—we still stand in awe of the pioneers who, with nothing but their faith, courage, and primitive technology, blazed the trails and laid the foundations of modern America.

Merrill J. Mattes
Littleton, Colorado

Site Locations

1 Westport Landing
2 Independence Square
3 Ft. Leavenworth
4 Weston
5 Old Ft. Kearny
6 Kanesville
7 Winter Quarters
8 Alcove Spring
9 Hollenberg Ranch
10 Rock Creek
11 Pawnee Village
12 Ft. Kearny
13 South Platte Crossing
14 California Hill
15 Ash Hollow
16 Courthouse Rock
17 Chimney Rock

18 Scotts Bluff and Mitchell Pass
19 Ft. Laramie
20 Register Cliff and Oregon Trail Ruts
21 Laramie Peak
22 Red Hills
23 Sidley Peak-Black Hills
24 Deer Creek
25 Ft. Casper
26 Independence Rock
27 Sweetwater Pass and Devil's Gate
28 Old Man-Sweetwater
29 Three Crossings
30 First View
31 Rocky Ridge
32 Twin Mounds
33 Pacific Spring
34 South Pass Area

35 Plume Rock and Dry Sandy
36 Lombard Ferry
37 Cathedral Rock-Church Butte
38 Bridger Butte
39 Ft. Bridger
40 Echo Canyon
41 Weber Canyon-Devil's Slide
42 Promised Land
43 Parley Canyon
44 Haystack Butte
45 Descent to Green
46 Fontenelle Bluffs
47 Case Ferry
48 Bear River Mountain Descent
49 Bear River Peak
50 Bear Mountain Sunrise
51 Soda Springs

52 Ft. Hall
53 Massacre Rocks
54 City of Rocks and Steeple Rock
55 Battle Mountain
56 Rabbit Hole Springs
57 Black Rock
58 Fremont's Castle
59 Fly Canyon
60 Singular Rock
61 Forty-Mile Desert
62 Donner Pass
63 Ft. Churchill
64 Mormon Station
65 Carson Canyon
66 Sutter's Fort
67 Sutter's Mill
68 Placerville

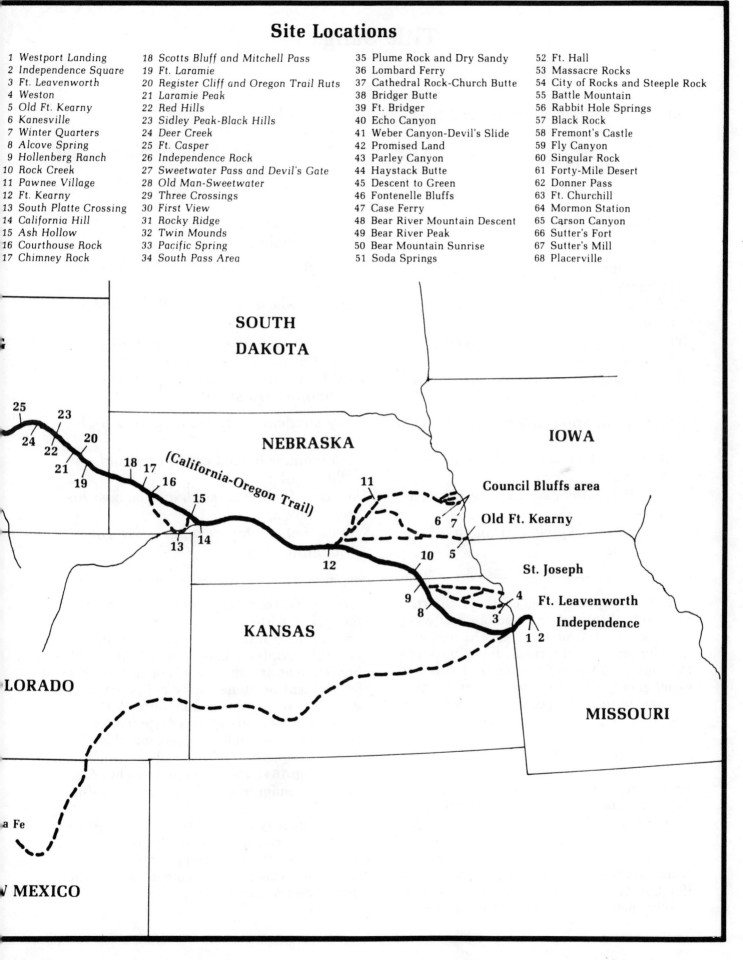

Title Song

Oh, don't you remember Sweet Betsey
   from Pike,
Who cross'd the big mountains with her
   lover Ike,
With two yoke of cattle, a large yellow
   dog,
A tall Shanghai rooster and one spotted
   hog.

They soon reached the desert, where
   Betsey gave out,
And down in the sand she lay rolling
   about;
While Ike, half-distracted, looked on
   with surprise,
Saying, "Betsey, get up, you'll get sand
   in your eyes."

Their wagon broke down with a terrible
   crash,
And out on the prairie rolled all kinds
   of trash;
A few little baby clothes done up with
   care—
'Twas rather suspicious, though all on
   the square

The Shanghai ran off, and their cattle
   all died;
That morning the last piece of bacon was
   fried;
Poor Ike was discouraged, and Betsey got
   mad;
The dog drooped his tail and looked
   wondrously sad.

Sweet Betsey got up in a great deal of
   pain,
Declared she'd go back to Pike County
   again;
But Ike gave a sigh and they fondly
   embraced,
And they travelled along with his arm
   round her waist.

They suddenly stopped on a very high
   hill,
With wonder looked down upon old
   Placerville;
Ike sighed when he said, and he cast his
   eyes down,
"Sweet Betsey, my darling, we've got to
   Hangtown."

In this popular song of the California emigrants there can be found much of what the trek to California was like. The song was both humerous and serious, describing both the emigrants themselves and the hardships experienced on their two thousand-mile journey to their "El Dorado," or for Betsey and Ike, "Hangtown" as Placerville was often called.

The emigrants were hardy individuals with a dream of a better life, full of adventure, and a drive for self-preservation. They were resourceful when they needed to be and thankful when their trek was over.

Their journey was long and tiresome. The first half was usually the easiest, but the second half—there came the mountains, then the deserts, and then more mountains, until finally they reached their goal, California!

First would come the sun and the heat, then the lack of water and the sand. For the late-coming emigrants or stragglers it could also be the winter snows and the cold. Breakdowns and the loss of materials either by accident or by necessity to lighten their loads caused many a hardship. With the exhaustion of food supplies despair often set in, but if these could be overcome their "El Dorado" could still be reached.

Between 1841 and 1860 about two hundred thousand emigrants trod the trail to California.

This book is a brief history of the early California Trail and a pictorial journey along it from both the eyes and pens of the early emigrants along with photographs of the corresponding areas today.

Preface

California has lured people for more than one hundred forty years. For some it has been a place to start a new life and to raise a family, while for others it has been a place to find or make a fortune to bring back to their family or to use for themselves. For me the lure hasn't been California itself, but the route to California that these early dreamers and adventurers had taken.

I can remember as a boy standing in front of a sign by the road describing the terrible hardships experienced on the Forty-Mile Desert and wondering how the emigrants ever made it. About fifteen years ago on a return trip from California I came across another sign different from the one I remembered as a boy, but still about the Forty-Mile Desert. Reading it, it helped rekindle my interest in the trails west and the emigrants that took them. As a history teacher I had a professional interest, but it was my personal interest and curiosity that became the motivating force behind my various journeys along the many trails since that trip. I hoped I could come to understand not only the hardships but also the feelings these early emigrants and gold-seeking "argonauts" experienced more than one hundred years ago as they traveled west on the trails.

For the past fifteen years I have spent much of my spare time reading the diaries and journals of emigrants and the various guidebooks, which became available to the emigrants as the years passed and the trails developed, and looking at the drawings and sketches made by the emigrants on their westward treks. Parts of my summers were then spent locating the various sites that were mentioned or drawn by the emigrants in their diaries. I hoped that by finding and writing about them I could help in my own way to preserve their experiences so they would be available for others in the future.

In recent years two important events have occurred that have helped save our trails west for future generations. First, there was the formation of new organizations to preserve the trails. The most recent and largest of these is called the Oregon-California Trails Association (OCTA, Box 42, Gerald, Missouri 63037). It has as its major goal the identification, preservation, and improved interpretation of the emigrant trails and related historical sites. This organization is proving to be both an effective and educational organization, attracting the attention and participation of both interested laymen and scholars alike. It has successfully encouraged the markings of various sites along the main and alternate routes of the Oregon and California trails and has helped preserve sections of the trails from being destroyed by new roads and pipelines. Two other organizations, which predate it by a decade, are Trails West, Inc., and the Nevada Emigrant Trails Marking Committee of the Nevada Historical Society; both are dedicated to identifying and preserving the old trails and have done an outstanding job.

The other important development has been the establishment by Congress of the Oregon National Historic Trail and authorization for a study expected to lead to similar recognition of the California Trail. Thus, the federal government has become more committed to recognizing and preserving these old highways themselves, as well as a few old forts and landmarks already preserved by the National Park Service.

For future tourists and scholars of the West these two developments will help preserve for them the way west that our earlier relatives and countrymen took. Further, in the years ahead it will now be possible for many travelers to experience something of what the trek was like.

This book will introduce you to the California Trail and the emigrant experience. Other books go into much greater detail about the events and the people, but this one will let you "sample" the trail—to hear, see and feel what the way west was like.

Come join the author and "Betsey and Ike" on a journey west like you've never taken before.

Introduction

The route to California and the California Trail are not synonymous. While the focus of this book will be the main overland route to California, there were other ways of getting to California that also deserve to be discussed because during certain years they were used more heavily than the main overland route.

First, however, let's examine the general route of the main California Trail. The eastern half of the trail coincided with that of the Oregon Trail. Its origins were the different "jumping-off" or embarking places along the Missouri River. Over the years the major embarking areas changed. Starting in 1841 it would have been Independence, Missouri, but soon other cities such as Westport, Ft. Leavenworth, Weston, St. Joseph, Old Fort Kearny/Nebraska City, and Kanesville or the Council Bluffs area became the centers. The name of the particular route used by emigrants usually derived from the city of its origin—such as the Independence Road or the St. Joe Road. Because of the heavy use by the Mormons in the area around Kanesville or Council Bluffs, the trail starting there and following the northside of the Platte River is sometimes called the Mormon Trail. It should be noted that it was used earlier by trappers, and later also by thousands of non-Mormon emigrants. In fact, research by *one historian* suggests that at least one-third of all central overland emigrants used this northern route, also known as the Council Bluffs Road. All these starting routes soon combined to form one main braid near Grand Island, Nebraska, just east of where Fort Kearny was built.

Here at the confluence of the different routes the emigrants traveled on both sides of the Platte River and then along the North Platte River. Near Casper, Wyoming, the emigrants left the North Platte and cut over to the Sweetwater River. Over the years of emigration many parallel routes were developed. Although they might weave a little from year to year, they all followed the "corridor" formed by these three river valleys. And all were headed for and funneled through the great South Pass.

Once through the pass the California emigrants and argonauts, again had a choice of routes, depending on the year they traveled the trail. Some continued on the Oregon Trail to Fort Bridger and then north to Fort Hall and west along the Snake River until they cut off the Oregon Trail in the vicinity of the Raft River and crossed over to the Humboldt or Mary's River. Others would cut off the dip to Fort Bridger by using the Greenwood or Sublette Cutoff or many of the minor ones that soon developed in that region and then head for Fort Hall. Still others would later try the Hudspeth or Myers, Cutoff before reaching Fort Hall. Some even went to Fort Bridger and then tried the Hastings Cutoff or followed the Mormon or Salt Lake route to the Humboldt. By 1859 the emigrants even had another route to use—the Lander Road. It cut off before South Pass at the Burnt Ranch and ended up near Fort Hall. No matter which route the emigrants used they all finally ended up somewhere along the Mary's or Humboldt River in Nevada.

As on the eastern half of the trail the emigrants were again funneled along a river, and a maze of trails developed along the Humboldt. Most emigrants followed it until the river "gave out" in the area known as "Humboldt's Sink." But as with earlier sections of the trail various routes were soon developed that offered the emigrants a choice of routes for the last segment of their journey, depending again on the year of the emigration. The three major ones were the Truckee, the Carson, and the Lassen routes, which terminated near Sutter's Fort and the "Gold Fields." But soon even these had their splinter routes, and many of them will be identified later in the history section of this book.

Many emigrants used other routes. Some turned southward from Salt Lake City to follow the Old Spanish Trail (originating in Santa Fe) that led to Los Angeles. Others went southwestward from Santa Fe to get on the Gila River route to Los Angeles. In 1849

James Wilkins was on his way to California along the Platte when he met some wagons coming east. After inquiring they told him they were returning to take the Santa Fe Trail because they were afraid that with all the emigrants ahead of them on the main trail there would not be enough grass left for their own stock. Some emigrants tried a new cutoff from the Salt Lake-Los Angeles Road and went through an area that came to be called "Death Valley" because of all the suffering that faced the emigrants there. Briefly then, these were some of the other overland routes that were used by some of the emigrants.

The following statistics taken from John Unruh's *The Plains Across*, University of Illinois Press show the number of emigrants by year that came to California by the overland route:

1841	34	1851	1,100
1842	0	1852	50,000
1843	38	1853	20,000
1844	53	1854	12,000
1845	260	1855	1,500
1846	1,500	1856	8,000
1847	450	1857	4,000
1848	400	1858	6,000
1849	25,000	1859	17,000
1850	44,000	1860	9,000

Thus, it seems that about two hundred thousand emigrants went overland to California, and another one hundred thousand went to Oregon and Utah during this same twenty-year period.

In addition to the overland routes there were still other ways to California, which during some years proved to be more popular with the emigrants and argonauts. These were the sea routes. By booking passage on a sailing ship or steamer one of several routes could be used. The most popular was the all-water route around Cape Horn totaling about thirteen thousand nautical miles. The others were also by water, but with intermediate land crossings of Panama, Nicaragua, or Mexico. The longest, the Panama route, was over five thousand miles. These routes had been used by the Spanish merchants and navy since colonial days to get to California, but it was the U.S. interest in California and then the discovery of gold that brought about the fuller development of these routes, especially the Panama route.

Because of the popularity of the sea routes with many of the California argonauts during the gold rush period an examination and comparison of them with the overland route with their respective problems should be considered.

The emigrants who used the overland route as opposed to the sea route tended to come from different areas and socioeconomic groups. Generally the sea routes were more expensive than the overland route. The per passenger cost started at about $150 but averaged about $300 for the trip around the Horn. The total cost of the trip by way of Panama was about $455, but during the gold rush years tickets were frequently sold by "scalpers" for three times as much or more, and they were readily purchased. This cost included not only the passage but also the food during the voyage. Because of the higher costs the sea route tended to be used by wealthier people such as doctors, lawyers, businessmen, and other professionals. The passengers also tended to come from the coastal and urban areas, especially the Northeast with New York City as the main port. For the average rural family, the total cost was prohibitive, yet a single person might use it.

The overland route was largely taken by the interior or rural families and tended to have a lower per capita cost. It is true that many professional people traveled on the trails, but they tended to come from the interior lands. The many single men who went overland during the gold rush frequently signed on with a wagon company and paid from $50.00 to $150.00 depending on the work arrangements made with the leader. The typical farm family averaged between four to six people and traveled by wagon. It is a little more difficult to figure costs for the overland route, but by using various guidebooks a good basis can be found. Depending on the specific type and number of draft animals used—oxen, mules, or horses—total costs can be given. Ware's 1849 guidebook put the total cost of wagon, teams, and supplies at $600.00 for ox teams and $670.78 for mule teams. Street's 1851 guidebook listed the estimated cost at $522.16 for ox teams and $600.00 for mule teams. By 1859 Marcy's guide listed $409.00 for an ox team and $809.00 for a mule team. Thus, by using the average number of emigrants, and the cost for wagon and team, it seems that the cost of individual transportation was between $100 and $200. Hopefully the emigrant still had some stock and their wagon when they arrived in California, and this reduced their net cost even more. The wagon itself was a small farm or spring wagon, which cost between $80.00 to $85.00 while the cover or canvas might cost as much as $100.00. Each year as more improvements were made along the trail miscellaneous expenses for ferries and tolls tended to increase. Typical charges for ferries and bridges averaged from $3.00 to $6.00 per wagon and from twenty-five to fifty cents per animal. Yet, the actual charge varied greatly depending on what the operator thought they could extract from the emigrant. Some small bridges charged twenty-five cents per wagon while the most expensive was recorded at $16.00 at one Green River ferry. One emigrant put their extra expenses at $75.00, but suggested a family bring $150.00 to be sure.

There were perhaps three major advantages for the emigrants traveling by ship. First, they could leave at just about anytime of the year as long as voyages were scheduled. The most difficult part of the voyage was rounding the Horn, and it could be especially hard if the trip occurred during the Southern Hemisphere's winter months of July and August. The overland emigrants were restricted as far as when they could leave their jumping-off places because they could only leave late in spring when there was sufficient prairie grasses to sustain their livestock. If they left too early the grasses would not be out and their livestock would starve; in leaving too late there would be difficulty finding grass because earlier companies' stock had grazed the grasses away. Also if they left too late or traveled too slowly they chanced getting caught in the mountains during the winter snows as the Donner party did in 1846. Therefore, most

wagon companies left within four to six weeks of each other from April to May and were rarely out of contact or sight of other wagon companies, especially during the years of heavy overland traffic.

The second advantage of going by sea was that the emigrants could carry more supplies and equipment if they desired and wished to pay for it. The overland emigrant was limited by the size of their wagon and the number of people sharing it. The average number of people per wagon was four, depending on the year of emigration. Most of the early emigrants brought only one wagon and were lucky if they still had it when they arrived in California. By the early to mid-1850s emigrant families often recorded the provision of a second or perhaps a third vehicle for their trip. Other factors that ultimately played significant roles were the pretrip planning and the strength of their draft animals and their ability to last during the journey. Many an emigrant had to jettison some or all of their belongings before their journey was completed. A reporter for a St. Louis paper at Fort Kearny wrote that "soon it was found that the loading was too great for the teams, and now overboard goes everything. The road is lined with various articles—even gold vases and gold washers." Wilkins noted this about the Platte, "The road all along is strewed with old clothes boots provisions, particularly beans, I notice are left, and the wreck of wagons." At Fort Laramie he wrote that "a great many parties abandoning their wagons at this point and take to mule packing on account of rumours of no grass and bad rocky roads." Those who packed could carry even less than those with wagons. For those emigrants who kept their wagons many would finally be abandoned at the deserts when their animals gave out.

There was a third advantage for those emigrants who decided to cross the Isthmus of Panama and that was time. The trip at its fastest could take between one to two months, depending on the year the journey was made. In Street's guidebook of 1851 he listed the approximate time as forty-five days by steamer. It was the completion of the railroad across Panama by Wills Aspenwall by 1855 that drastically reduced the travel time from days to a few hours. The record for the route by way of Panama was twenty-one days in 1855. The trip around the Horn usually took less time than the overland journey, but some like the ship, *Apollo*, took as long as nine months, while the overland journey normally took between five and seven months. The record in 1849 was set by the *Greyhound* one of the new clipper-type ships, which made it in 112 days. In 1853 the *Northern Light* returned to New York from San Francisco in only 76 days. These were more the exception than the rule. By the early 1850s the average time for a clipper ship was about 132 days. Yet, as improvements were made all along the trail overland travel became faster and faster. In little more than a decade the time was nearly cut in half, and the route around the Horn began to lose its time advantage.

However, there were many problems that faced the oceangoing argonauts. Some were very similar to those experienced by the overland emigrants, but others were different.

Disease was one of the major problems that faced both the overland emigrants and those that went by sea. Cholera was the major killer on the California Trail during the years 1849, 1850 and 1852, taking an estimated two thousand or more lives each year. The disease also was contracted by those who came by sea. In 1849 people in Panama City were afflicted with it; it had come in with the gold seekers who then carried it to San Francisco. On his return voyage in 1852 Byron McKinstry noted that twelve deaths due to cholera occurred during the nine-day trip between Panama and New York. The people aboard ship could not keep separate from those with the disease or leave the ship. In 1855 one ship with 650 passengers lost 113 to cholera. Nevertheless, the disease never came close to killing the number of people aboard ship that it did on the overland route during the cholera outbreak's worst years. In fact, one estimate by Donald Jackson in his book *Gold Dust* put the total deaths at around fifty for all the sea voyages for 1849. More may have died in the cities, such as Panama City, however.

Smallpox was another feared disease and killer of emigrants on both land and sea. Other diseases such as yellow fever and malaria were especially dangerous for those crossing the Isthmus of Panama. In 1851 Borthwick crossed Panama, and he wrote that "there was here at this time a great deal of sickness, and absolute misery, among the Americans. Diarrhea and fever were the prevalent diseases."

One unique malady of the seagoing emigrants was seasickness, and it was the most common illness of all. It struck most passengers, especially at the outset of their journey. In 1852 Charles Harvey's first diary entry stated that the ship sailed from New York with "loud cheers" and "booming of cannons." The very next day, March 3, he noted that he "felt poorly eat verry little . . . good many passengers sick." Finally on March 8 he wrote, "Felt little better, eat little grewel." Even John Beach, son of the owner of the ship *Apollo*, suffered from it when only four days out of New York. Most people finally got accustomed to the normal rolling of the ship, and some passengers even likened it to the rolling of a wagon on the prairie.

Weather was a problem for all the emigrants. On the sea storms could increase the amount and severity of seasickness, but they could also be more troublesome. The storms at the Horn often caused ships, like the *Henry Lee*, to take as long as forty days to round it. Passengers often lashed themselves to their berths during bad weather. They were constantly soaked and hot food of any kind was impossible. J.D. Borthwick said during one gale "that boxes and chests of all sizes, besides casks of provisions and other ship's stores, which had got adrift, were cruising about promiscuously. . . . In the morning we found the cook's galley had fetched away, and the stove was rendered useless." That wasn't the only problem with winds and storms. In 1852 the *Grecian* lost her mizzen and fore topmast in a gale. In 1857 the ship *Central America* sunk and about 400 passengers were lost. Sometimes ships, such as the *Union* and *John A. Sutter*, ran aground.

At other times ships were forced to wait for a "fair wind." Charles Harvey's whole entry for one day was, "Dead calm," and on another, "Quite warm, The wind died away this morning and we are becalmed again water getting short provisions poor and a hot sun which makes it verry unpleasent and discourageing." The *Elizabeth* was becalmed in the extreme cold off Patagonia for nearly three weeks, and the *Apollo* waited almost two weeks west of San Francisco for a fair wind to take her into port.

For the overland emigrants the unpredictable prairie storms could bring torrential rains in minutes, which could flood rivers and backup river crossings for days, make the trail muddy or "heavy," or even flood them out. In 1850 George Keller reached the Ham's Fork but "found impossible to ford, on account of its swollen state." It took three days before they crossed and three attempts to construct a ferry strong enough. On the evening of June 13, 1853, James Woodworth had camped in a hollow for the evening. He wrote that the "wind bleu with great violence At the same time a terrible storm of rain accompanied with hard thunder came on . . . [the hollow] it soon filled to a depth of Six inches with water and all of the bedcloths were swimming in it We of course were obliged to evacuate the tent without ceremony and pass the night as best we could."

Just as the overland emigrants had problems with food, passengers aboard ship frequently complained about both the quantity and quality of food and the foul tasting water from the ship's caskets. On one voyage passengers complained that "there were two bugs for every bean" with their meals, but adding humerously that at least they had some fresh meat with their meals. By the end of the voyage they were frequently down to salt meat, beans, and hardtack. Mores Cogswell, a passenger bound for California on the *Sweden* wrote that "the beans are 3 to a quart of hot water, with a small piece of rusty pork." In 1860 Henry Huston on the steamer *Sonora* commented that some of the food was "'old enough to vote,' then 'roast beef' with a brown crust and all inside raw and bloody." The fish "all well rotted; Bread, Fruit and other solids come in about the same shape; Butter is here a liquid; tea and coffee are both nick-names, as those liquids very seldom have a taste of those vegetable, for which they are named." Water was often rationed and passengers on the *Grecian*

complained about the rationing of water by the cupfull.

On the overland trail food supplies were also down to a minimum by the time they reached the Humboldt and Carson sinks. James Wilkins wrote of the Pioneer Line, the first commercial wagon train to cross the plains, that "they like us had nothing left but bread and bacon." Finding freshwater supplies was also a problem because the springs and streams were frequently contaminated by human and animal wastes and dead carcasses. Further, on certain parts of the trail, such as the Sublette Cutoff, Salt Lake Desert, Black Rock Desert, and Forty-Mile Desert, good water was between forty to eighty miles away.

One disease usually associated with the sea voyages was scurvy. While records do indicate that some died they do not indicate that the problem was as severe as many first feared. It was, however, another problem that hit the overland emigrants. Wilkins wrote on September 19, 1849, "We are most of us taking the scurvey, myself amongst the rest. the gums bleed and the skin is becoming discoloured in patches." D.T. McCollum another emigrant on the trail noted that "nearly half the passengers in the Pioneer Line . . . have had the Scurvy, and four have died with it." Bruff wrote on September 30, 1849, "Much scurvy among the emigrants, a little girl's mouth badly affected with it." These accounts were expressed late in the journey of the emigrants. In 1850, however, George Keller did state that people were suffering from scurvy at Fort Laramie, which was much further east on the trail.

For the ocean voyagers there was not much in the way of sightseeing nor even the change of scenery, and boredom became a major problem. Yet, some well-organized groups were prepared. One from New York brought along a 150-volume library to read on their voyage. There probably wasn't much left of it once they arrived in San Francisco. On another ship Charles Harvey recorded that he passed much of his time by reading, playing euchre, jackstraws, hunting lice, and carving canes and rings. While some ships, such as the *Sweden*, sailed without stopping, most made one or two stops. On the Atlantic the ports were usually Rio de Janeiro or

Santa Catarina and on the Pacific, Talcahuano or Valparaiso. Brief as the stops were the passengers made the most of them. On the other hand, overland travelers frequently commented on the landscape and many took time to "sightsee" by looking at a gorge, or strange mound, or climbing rocks and carving their names on them.

While emigrants on the overland route had trouble finding camping grounds with sufficient grass and water they at least could sleep in the "wide open spaces." Passengers on ship were often overcrowded. The average size of a sailing ship in 1849 carried forty-eight argonauts plus crew and was ninety-three feet long and twenty-four feet abeam. This did not leave much room to roam. By the 1850s the new larger clipper ships could carry about three hundred passengers, but space was still tight. The early steamers could carry about two hundred passengers while by the late 1850s and early 1860s some carried seven hundred, but still space was scarce. The first steamer from Panama City, the *California*, was forced to take on board 365 passengers while it was built for only 215 after the gold seekers had threatened the captain. Even on regular voyages sleeping quarters were crowded. Sleeping births were often tiered— three abreast two feet apart one on top of the other. Passengers on the *Alexander Von Humboldt* were nine to a compartment—a six-foot square. One could only imagine what the aroma must have been like after months at sea or after stormy weather.

One last problem for the oceangoing emigrants was that there were fire and explosions on steamers. Although fire was a very rare occurrence, the ship *Independence* burned in 1853 and 125 out of 300 passengers died. For the overland emigrant their major problem with fire was getting enough wood, sage, or buffalo chips for their cooking fires. Often they would make use of a discarded wagon as a fuel supply. One has often heard of great prairie fires facing emigrants, but there just aren't many records to substantiate them. This is probably due to the fact that when the emigrants were on the plains it was spring and the grasses were short and green. By the time they were traveling during the drier months of summer they were traveling in the desert or drier areas of the trail where there was little vegetation to burn.

These then were some of the difficult realities facing the oceangoing emigrants and their overland counterparts. Despite the problems traveling by sea proved to be extremely popular after gold was discovered in 1848. San Francisco had welcomed only two U.S. ships in 1848, but in 1849 over 775 ships brought the argonauts. More people came by ship in 1849 than came by wagon. The estimates range form a low of over 22,000 to a high of 40,000 emigrants by ship, while about 6,200 wagons moved between 21,000 and 23,000 emigrants to California.

Early History of the California Trail

1818-21

The Mexican War for independence from Spain was started by Father Miguel Hidalgo y Costilla. Formal independence for Mexico was finally granted and signed in 1821.

1819

The Adams-Onis Treaty was signed with Spain. This set the northern boundary of the Mexican Territory as the forty-second parallel to the Continental Divide. The area directly north of it was the Oregon Territory and was claimed by the United States, Great Britain, and Russia. Russia still had an outpost in California, Fort Ross, which it had set up and dedicated on September 10, 1812. They would later sell it to John Sutter.

1821

After the Mexican independence U.S. interests in California began to increase. At first it was a merchant venture with interests in shipping cattle hides and sea otter skins back east. Later Americans would come to the California area in hopes of starting a new life or finding gold.

1824

Tom Fitzpatrick and other trappers are said to have camped at Independence Rock and celebrated the Fourth of July there. Some sources also credit Fitzpatrick with naming the rock. This large granite rock would become a major landmark on the overland trails to California and Oregon. Father DeSmet later called this rock the "Great Register of the Desert" because of all the names written and carved on it by those who visited it—both trapper and emigrant alike.

1826

Joseph Robidoux set up a trading post near the banks of the Missouri River. The site was to become the city of St. Joseph.

Jedediah Smith, the famous mountain man, led a party of trappers to California and the San Gabriel Mission. He was looking for new beaver grounds and also hoping to find the mythical San Buenaventura River, which would open the Rocky Mountains up to oceangoing ships. In entering Mexican California he broke the law, was put in jail, and then released on the promise that he would leave California by the same way he entered. He started to leave but then hunted and set up a stockade on the Stanislaus River. While some of his men remained he left for the Rendezvous at Bear Lake and returned to California when it was over. He was jailed and then released again on the promise to leave and not return. This time he headed north to the Oregon Territory. Other trappers such as Sylvester Pattie had similar problems with the Mexican officials.

The route Smith used to enter California was not well documented, but there is little evidence that it was used by later emigrants. However, a river where they camped while going north did come to be known as the "American River," and this does become important in California's history.

1827

The town of Independence, Missouri, was founded. It became the jumping-off place for the Santa Fe Trail and later the California and Oregon trails. The first wagon company left for California from Independence in 1841. Independence Square and the courthouse marked the beginning of the trails. It was the springs in the area that made Independence a natural location for both the town and the trails.

Fort Leavenworth was established by the military on the Missouri River. It provided protection for the Santa Fe Trail. During the years of the early gold rush in California it served as another of the jumping-off centers for the emigrants.

1828

Hiram Scott, a trapper, was left by his companions and disappeared. The following year William Sublette found a skeleton that was believed to have been Scott's. The bluffs along that section of the Platte River were named for him. Over the years different stories developed about who Hiram Scott was and how he came to die. As early as 1830 the first written record of the legend was made by Warren Ferris.

1828-36

Andrew Jackson was elected president of the United States, and he shortly began negotiations with Mexico to purchase California and New Mexico. After six years the negotiations broke off. Succeeding presidents continued to try to obtain California.

1833

John C. McCoy founded the town of Westport a few miles west of Independence. Once Westport Landing was developed on the Missouri the two areas grew together and it also became another jumping-off place for the emigrant trail.

1833-34

Joseph Walker, another famous trapper and mountain man, traveled from the Salt Lake region down the Mary's or Humboldt River. He crossed the Sierra Nevada down near their southern end at a pass that now bears his name, Walker Pass. While his whole route was not used by the emigrants, many traveled on certain parts of it. In 1869 the transcontinental railroad also used parts of it.

1834

Some believe that Kit Carson and other trappers were the pathfinders for the route down the Raft River to Goose Creek and over to Bishop's Creek, headwaters of the Mary's or Humboldt River. He then traveled part way down the Humboldt River along the same general route used earlier by Walker and then returned. Trappers now used this route to hunt beavers in the upper part of the Mary's River. This route later became the main branch of the California Trail from Fort Hall.

Fort William was constructed near the mouth of the Laramie River on the North Platte by Robert Campbell, William Sublette's co-partner. This fort was visited by Alfred J. Miller, painter for Sir William Drummond Stewart, in 1837, he was on a "tour" of the American West. Miller's paintings of the fort are the only ones that exist of the fort and are well-known today. The fort changed owners many times during the next few years, and finally a new fort replaced it in 1841 just in time for the development of the California-Oregon trails.

Nathaniel J. Wyeth contracted to sell supplies at the Rendezvous, but by the time he arrived there others were already selling supplies to the mountain men. Wyeth decided to construct a fort on the Snake River and it was called Fort Hall. In 1837 it was sold to the Hudson's Bay Company, and they enlarged it from its original size to about eighty by one hundred twenty feet. In 1856 the fort was abandoned, and by 1862 it had succumbed to the flooding of the Snake. The fort served as the last major resupply area for the California-bound emigrants who did not take the many cutoffs that developed earlier along the trail.

1836

The first California revolution for independence was led by a native-born Californios, Juan Bautista Alvarado and Jose Castro. Alvarado's proclamation of independence on November 7, 1836, was supported by thirty U.S. and British frontiersmen. However, when the Mexican government appointed Alvarado the legitimate governor of California he ended the rebellion. In 1846 Castro was planning another rebellion against Mexico, but the American supported Bear Flag Revolt swept by him.

John Marsh arrived in California. He was an adventurer, trapper, storekeeper, former Indian agent, and finally a major landowner in California. He left Missouri for California when threatened with arrest for selling guns illegally to the Indians. Once in California he set up a practice as a physician. Shortly thereafter he obtained a large rancho of about fifty thousand acres on San Francisco

Bay. His rancho became one of the objectives for many of the later California emigrants. He also actively encouraged Americans to come to California.

1837

Joseph Moore founded the Missouri River town of Weston. For a few years in the 1850s it rivaled Independence and St. Joseph as a jumping off place. James Wilkins disembarked here in 1849. By 1860 Weston's boom period was over.

1839

John Sutter arrived in California. He originally left Switzerland to escape a jail sentence, came to the United States and then journeyed to Oregon in 1838, traveling with a party of missionaries. He went to California by way of Hawaii and Alaska. He was another adventurer like Marsh and soon became another large landowner. He persuaded Governor Alvarado to grant him eleven square miles of land, about forty-seven thousand acres, and finally obtained two more large land grants. He promised the governor to set up a colony of Swiss to serve as a buffer between the Americans, British, Russians, and the Mexicans. His colony of "New Helvetia" was at the junction of the American and Sacramento rivers. There he built his fort which became the headquarters for his empire of the future—Sutter's Fort; it became the desired destination for Americans who came over the California Trail. Today Sutter's Fort has been restored and reconstructed and can be visited.

The two ranches of John Marsh and John Sutter soon developed into the end of the trail for the pre-gold rush emigrants. They served as a resupply depot for the emigrants who succeed in arriving in California and needed materials to start their new lives. For the early years of the trail they also served as a base station for rescue missions for emigrants needing help back on the trail. The parties that finally rescued the remnants of the Donner party left from Fort Sutter. Thus, for the California emigrants, these two ranches played a role similar to that played by the Lee and Whitman missions and Fort Vancouver for the Oregon emigrants.

John Bidwell, a member of the Western Emigration Society, tried to get people interested in traveling to California. His work, plus that by others such as John Marsh and the old trapper Robidoux, had stirred the interests of people in Missouri, Arkansas, Illinois, and Kentucky. By the winter of 1840 plans were made by many of them to meet in Independence by May 9, 1841, to start their trek to California.

1840

British and Americans at home and in California increased their agitation for a takeover of the Mexican state of California.

1841

The old wooden Fort William was abandoned and replaced by another structure made out of adobe and called Fort John. Most emigrants along the trail called it Fort Laramie as they did the earlier Fort William. Laramie Peak is the predominant geographical feature in that area and served as a landmark for travelers in that area. The new fort was about 123 feet by 168 feet. Francis Parkman, a young adventurer and writer stayed there in 1846 and gives one of the best descriptions of the fort itself. He stated that "the little fort is built of bricks dried in the sun . . . of oblong form, with bastions of clay . . . at two of the corners. . . . The walls are about fifteen feet high." This was a major stopping place for the emigrants and it signified the completion of the prairie portion of their journey.

The Russians voluntarily left Fort Ross and with it their interests in California. They had already agreed in 1824 not to expand their interests below fifty-four degrees, forty minutes north. John Sutter purchased the fort from the Russians and its role in California history was over. Fort Ross has also been restored and reconstructed and can be visited today.

This was the year that the U.S. emigrants began to arrive in California over what ultimately developed into the California Trail. There were three groups—one from Oregon, including women and children; another from New Mexico, following the caravan trail to Los Angeles; and the third, the Bidwell party. This latter group were the first emigrants to travel across the Sierra Nevada to John Marsh's ranch and then to Sutter's Fort along the general route that came to be known as the California Trail.

The party of emigrants met in May in Independence, Missouri, as had been previously decided. It was comprised of sixty-nine people. The company has been called the Bartleson-Bidwell party. They luckily were able to join a party of missionaries, including the famous Father DeSmet who was being guided by Thomas Fitzpatrick and Joseph Meek. They followed what was to be called the Oregon-California Trail. West of Soda Springs the company divided. Thirty-four emigrants continued with the missionaries on the Oregon Trail to Fort Hall and then to Oregon, while thirty-five turned south to break open a route to California. While the complete route they took was not followed by later emigrants parts of it were to be used. Nancy Kelsey and her baby, Ann, were the first woman and child on the California Trail. One of the camping places they stopped at in Utah they called Rabbit Spring, and it is still known by that name today. They faced great hardships crossing the Great Salt Lake Desert and finally after moving southwest found a pass, Harrison Pass, in the Ruby Mountains and crossed over to the Mary's or Humboldt River. They were forced to abandon their wagons before crossing the mountains and thus continued their journey by foot and pack animals. After following the Mary's River they continued south to the Walker River and crossed the Sierra Nevada at or near the Sonora Pass. These were the first emigrants, but because they left their wagons the first successful wagon company would have to wait a few more years. Also not until 1852 was the probable pass they used, used again by other emigrants.

1842

John Frémont, guided by Kit Carson, headed out from Westport to South Pass and the Rocky Mountains. With his cartographer, Charles Preuss, they mapped the trail and recorded information, which became very useful to emigrants who used the route. A few years later they completed the route all the way to Oregon and publish-ed their reports, which were widely known and read in the late 1840s.

No emigrant wagon companies left for California in 1842, but companies left for Oregon and, thus, developed the first half of the trail. About twelve of the men who went west to California in 1841 returned to the States, trying to find a better route while also using part of their 1841 trail. They were led by Chiles and Hopper. Many of the members of this party became important to the history of California and the trail. Creeks, rivers, towns, lakes, mountains, and forts were named after these hardy emigrants. Many also became guides for later emigrant companies and helped to open new routes and will be noted later in this book.

President Tyler tried again to negotiate with Mexico to obtain California. However, his efforts failed when a brash Commodore Jones "captured" Monterey on October 19, thinking war with Mexico had broken out. As a result the Mexicans became even more suspicious of the United States.

1842-43

Jim Bridger and Louis Vasquez built a trading post near the Black's Fork of the Green River. It was on the bluffs but was later moved to the bottomland. This trading post became a major stopping and resupply area for the early emigrants and for the later ones who used the Salt Lake Road or cutoff to California. For those emigrants who took any of the different cutoffs, such as the Greenwood or Sublette, Slate Creek, Kinney, Baker-Davis, or Lander Road, the fort was bypassed. Brigham Young purchased the fort or post in 1855, but it was abandoned and burned in 1857. The U.S. Army constructed a new fort on the old location almost immediately. Today parts of the old military fort have been restored and reconstructed, and it is a living museum and state historic site.

1843

St. Joseph, Missouri, was laid out on the site of the earlier trading post. It soon developed into another of the major embarking areas for the westward emigrants. It also became the eastern terminus of the short-lived Pony Express in 1860.

Joseph Chiles organized a wagon company to return with him to California. Even though he had not succeeded with wagons in 1841, he decided to try again with them. The party included about eight wagons and thirty people—many were friends and relatives, including women and children of people already in California. His wagon company traveled behind the "Great Migration" of the emigrants to Oregon and also behind John C. Frémont who was on another of his trips of exploration to Oregon. His return to the States from Oregon would bring Frémont through California. Chiles's party followed the already defined route of the Oregon Trail as it was called then, all the way to Fort Hall. There he decided to divide the company. Joseph Walker led the largest group with the women and children and the wagons, while Chiles took some of the men and led a pack train on a different route. Walker turned off the Oregon Trail at Calder Creek, cut over to the Raft River, then to the City of the Rocks, and down to the Mary's River. The original plan called for Walker to meet Chiles near the Humboldt Sink after he had successfully entered California from the north and found a new route across the Sierra Nevada. However, Chiles wasn't there and Walker headed south along the route he had taken back in 1834. About five hundred miles of the route Walker established, from the Raft River to the Humboldt Sink, became the major route of the California Trail. As for Chiles his route had continued west along the Oregon Trail until finally reaching Fort Boise. A little west of there he cut southwest finally picking up the Sacramento River and more or less followed it to Sutter's Fort. This route proved to be as poor as the other. Walker's party had been forced to abandon their wagons near Owens Lake, and thus, it would take another year before wagons would make it all the way across the Sierra Nevada and into California.

1844

This year Frémont completed his exploration and mapping of the route to Oregon that he had begun in 1842. Frémont decided to return to the United States by heading south into California. By February he made it to Sutter's Fort. This venture into Mexican territory by members of the U.S. Army made Mexico nervous. Fremont claimed he needed fresh horses for his journey to cross the Sierra Nevada. He then returned to the United States, mapping his route all the way. While this route was not used by the emigrants, his maps showed that the lands between the Rocky and Sierra Nevada formed a "Great Basin." He would return again to California in 1845, giving names to a number of places and changing the Mary's River named earlier by Peter Skene Ogden of the Hudson's Bay Company to the Humboldt River. The Carson River was named for his scout, Kit Carson, and the entrance to San Francisco was later named the "Golden Gate."

Peter Lassen, a Dane, obtained a land grant from the Mexican government about one hundred miles north of Sutter's Fort on the Sacramento River. Lassen had come to California by way of Oregon in 1839-40 and had hoped to create an empire like Sutter's, and to get rich off the new emigrants. His chance would come in a few years.

This was the year that the first wagon company made it over the Sierra Nevada, establishing at last a usable wagon route. It was led by Elisha Stephens who served as captain. The Stephens-Townsend-Murphy party, as it is often called, set off from Council Bluffs, Iowa, in March 1844. It was comprised of twenty-three men, eight women, and fifteen children. Caleb Greenwood and his sons acted as pilots for the first half of the trail. It followed the established Oregon Trail as far as South Pass. Shortly thereafter they decided to try a new cutoff. Isaac "Old Man" Hitchock suggested that they cut west instead of heading southwest to Fort Bridger and thereby save some time. It seemed that Hitchock knew generally of the route and that it may have been used by Bonneville in 1832 but not since then. The company discussed it and voted to try it. While it proved drier and longer than originally thought, all made it safely across. In fact part of the company returned back over the route to the Big Sandy to look for cattle that had been lost and then returned to cross it again. This route came to be called the Greenwood

Cutoff and, later, the Sublette Cutoff. After crossing the Bear Mountains they headed north toward Fort Hall. Shortly after leaving Fort Hall they cut across and followed Walker's route all the way down the Humboldt. At the Humboldt Sink and the "Forty-Mile Desert," as it is called later, they came in contact with an Indian called Truckee. He told them of a stream and passage west across the desert. They crossed over to it and followed it up into the mountains. Today the river still bears the name given it by the thankful emigrants as does a meadow area, respectively the Truckee River and Truckee Meadows, the present site of Reno. From there the emigrants crossed at what later is called Donner's Pass and Donner Creek down the west side of the moutains. While they were forced to temporarily leave their wagons at various places along the trail and some of the emigrants were even forced to spend part of the winter in cabins they built, they all arrived safely by the spring of 1845. In addition to the first use of the Greenwood Cutoff and bringing the first wagons to California, two children were born along the way Ellen Independence Miller near Independence Rock and Elizabeth Yuba Murphy near Yuba Creek.

Lansford Hastings left California by sea for the East, hoping to encourage emigration to California and to publish a guidebook. His guidebook would contain the infamous Hastings Cutoff, the route taken by the ill-fated Donner party in 1846, but only vaguely described and never traveled by Hastings. He had originally gone to Oregon in 1842 and then left after not finding what he had hoped for and decided that California was the better place to make his fortune.

1845

James K. Polk became president and pledged himself to obtain California for the United States. His plan was three pronged. First, he hoped to obtain it by direct negotiations and purchase. Second, by encouraging independence movements in California by pledging to protect any Americans seeking to make California part of the United States. As a result, Secretary of State Buchanan instructed Consul Larkin to "arouse in their bosoms that love of liberty

and independence so natural to the American continent," and that "if the People should desire to unite their destiny with ours, they would be received as brethren." Polk's third plan was war if all else failed.

More wagon companies headed for California. This year St. Joseph was the major embarking area. Again the companies included women and children. Lansford Hastings headed for California, but he traveled by horse not wagon. A more unfortunate first is recorded this year—the first death of an emigrant by an Indian. A man called Pierce was killed on the Truckee River. It should be noted that perhaps part of the blame could be placed on the actions of John Greenwood and Sam Kinney who in 1844 had earlier started trouble with the Indians along the Humboldt. From this year on the Indians, especially the "Diggers" as they were frequently called, became more of a problem, but the major problems facing the emigrants still remained time, distance, food, deserts, and winter.

1845-6

John C. Frémont left on his third official journey of exploration. He explored and traveled through much of the territory along the California Trail, but most of it was not related to the trail and would have little impact on the emigrants route. He would, however, play a larger role in the California revolt, and this would ultimately impact on his career. Walker and Carson acted as his guides during the journey.

1846

This was a major year for both the history of the California Trail and for California because of the revolt and its impact, the continued emigration, and the events surrounding some of the companies.

By December 1845 Frémont was back in California with a larger and stronger military and scientific force than he had had previously in 1844. Having narrowly avoided a conflict with the Mexicans, he left for Oregon. However, in May he was overtaken by a Marine Corps courier, Lt. Archibald Gillespie, and after discussions he returned to California in time for the California Revolt. Even today there is still much

13

speculation about what exactly transpired during their meeting and what instructions, if any, Frémont received from Gillespie. Events began to move rapidly, but it must be noted that communications were not as fast as today's. On April 25 Mexican troops had opened fire on General Zachary Taylor's forces at the Rio Grande, and on May 11 President Polk sent a War Message to Congress. Back in California the Americans continued their agitation and William B. Ide, a former schoolteacher, proclaimed California an independent republic, the Bear Flag Republic, on June 14, 1846, at Sonora. Frémont came to the aid of the Americans. Commodore Sloat landed in Monterey on July 7, and the Bear Flag Republic was dissolved and the California fighters joined the U.S. Army as the California Volunteers under Fremont. On July 9, Captain John Montgomery landed in San Francisco and the American flag was raised. While fighting still continued in places the Mexican forces capitulated, and the campaign was over on January 13, 1847, when Frémont and Andies Pico signed an agreement. The formal treaty came in another year.

A large company of Mormons, 238 emigrants, arrived from New York by ship with Sam Brannan as their leader on July 31, 1846. There had been discussions earlier by the Mormons about making California their "Promised Land." However, by the time they arrived Brigham Young had already decided on the Great Salt Lake Valley. Yet, Sam Brannan and these Mormons would still play an important role in the development of California and the California Trail.

Levi Scott and Jesse Applegate opened the Applegate Trail to Oregon. This route left the main route along the Snake River cutting over to the Humboldt, leaving it to cross the Black Rock Desert, and then entering Oregon from the south. The cutoff from the Humboldt was later incorporated into part of the Lassen route in 1848 and played a major role in 1849.

While the political status of California was being resolved, another great crisis was developing that has come to be almost synonymous with the California Trail and the hardships faced by the emigrants—the Donner disaster.

The Donner party has been one of the last parties to leave Independence in 1846. Almost from the beginning it seemed to be haunted by delays and problems. At Alcove Spring in Kansas they experienced their first death, that of Grandmother Keyes. This, however, was not to be their last. Today a marker can be found there, but it is a recent one and a couple hundred feet from the actual grave site, which is near or directly under the county road. Here also can be found the stone carved by James Reed with his initials and name. He would play a central role later in the journey. Also carved in the rocks is the name "Alcove Spring," given by Edwin Bryant and carved by George McKinstry, also members traveling together at that time. (See photos of carvings in photo section.)

The Donner party had heard of the Hastings Cutoff and were planning on taking it. However, long before getting to Fort Bridger where they would have to leave the main trail they were warned by James Clyman, a famous mountain man and friend of James Reed, that there was no trail there and that they should not try it, but rather should continue along the established route by way of Fort Hall. However, once at the fort, Jim Bridger seemed to indicate that it was possible. Yet, in reality it had never been tried by wagons. Even the route to Salt Lake had not previously been used as such. Hastings had already started with other wagons to try his new route and was reportedly ready to help guide the Donners if they could catch up. The Donners and some others decided to try it while others in the party decided to follow the established route by way of Fort Hall. Those who took the established route to Fort Hall would reach California without any major problems. The Donners, however, were not able to catch up. They did send Reed ahead to find Hastings. He did, but Hastings would only "point out" a different and supposedly better route. This new route bypassed the Weber Canyon that the others had taken and crossed the Wasatch Mountains. As the Donners soon found out there was no trail there, and they had to cut their way through. This only delayed them more. Most of this new road would become part of the main route to Salt

Lake that the Mormons and others would follow in 1847 and later. Once they got to Salt Lake they had even more problems. Hastings had reported that the Salt Lake Desert was only about forty miles across, but in reality it was more like eighty miles to Pilot Peak. This was another major error of Hastings.

It now seemed that hardship and delays were constant companions of the Donners. Further down the trail in Nevada, Reed got into a fight with another member and killed him. He was almost executed but was forced out of the company and had to complete the journey on his own while his wife and family remained with the company. Reed finally made it safely to California and was one of the people to lead rescue parties to help the starving and stranded survivers that winter. By the time the Donner party reached the Truckee, winter was fast setting in. As they climbed the mountains they decided to rest. It was a fateful decision because snow fell and blocked the pass. They were forced to remain on the eastern side. They built cabins for protection hoping for a break in the weather which never came. They were soon out of food and none could be hunted. Some tried to get over the mountains on foot, but they were forced back. Starving and desperate with some members already dead and dying they turned to the only food supply they thought available—the bodies of those members who had already died. The rest is history. There are many books written on the subject for those interested in the complete history and story of their ordeal.

Earlier, while still on the desert, the Donners had sent two members ahead to Sutter's Fort to obtain additional supplies. There they learned that Reed had successfully made it to California, and they related the problems and delays that the Donners had experienced. Later, when the Donners did not show up, Reed and others realized that they were stranded in the mountains. But the California revolt had already started and this delayed rescue missions. By 1847 all those left alive were taken to California. Reed, himself, brought back members of his own family. Out of the Donner party forty members died and forty-seven members survived. It had been the worst disaster on

the California Trail. Today names such as Donner Pass, Donner Lake, and Donner Creek all commemorate the tragedy. Hastings was discredited and would never recover his honor and the Hastings Cutoff had seen its day.

1847

This was the year of the major Mormon migration to the Great Salt Lake Valley from the Council Bluffs/Omaha area under the leadership of Brigham Young. The Mormons stayed on the northern side of the Platte River, finally crossing over near Fort Laramie. The route used by the Mormons was later referred to by some as the Mormon Trail, even though much of it coincided with the main Oregon-California Trail. The Mormons opened important ferries to facilitate crossings of the Upper Platte and Green Rivers.

Only about ninety wagons headed for California this year and none tried the Hastings Cutoff.

Charles Hopper led the first company of twenty wagons over the route that cut off from the main Oregon Trail along the Snake River at the Raft River. Hopper had been with the Bartleson-Bidwell party in 1841 and Chiles in 1842. Other wagons followed the route cutting off at the Raft River, and this became the main route used from that time on.

1848

This year was a major turning point in the history of California and the California Trail. Many events would occur that would change the course of history, most notably the discovery of gold and the formal takeover of California by the United States.

On January 24, 1848, James Marshall discovered gold in the tailrace in a newly constructed mill on the American River. John Sutter, owner of the mill, wanted to keep it a secret until he could figure out just what to do about it. However, it was a secret that could not be kept. Stories were soon being told and finally on May 8, 1848, Sam Brannan reportedly shouted, "Gold! Gold! Gold on the American River!" on Montgomery Street in San Francisco and word spread like wildfire. Walter Colton alcalde of Monterey wrote, "The blacksmith dropped his hammer, the carpenter his plane, the mason his trowel, the farmer his sickle, the baker his loafs, and the tapster his bottle. All were off for the mines, some on horses, some on carts, some on crutches, and one went in a litter." The gold rush had started!

On February 2 the formal Treaty of Guadalupe Hildago ended the Mexican War. The areas we know of as California, Arizona, New Mexico, Nevada, and Utah were ceded to the United States.

This year also saw many changes in the trail itself. Military forts were being constructed and started to replace the fur company posts. Another route was opened around the Great Salt Lake and two new routes were opened across the Sierra Nevada to California.

The construction of a new fort near Grand Island on the Platte River showed the government's concern about the safety of the emigrants on their westward trek. At first it was called Fort Childs, but it was soon changed to Fort Kearny and replaced the Old Fort Kearny back east on the Missouri. It was built right on the trail and was to protect the emigrants who traveled along the Platte River. Lieutenant Woodbury was in charge of construction, and he had cottonwood trees planted around the parade ground. Today a few of those trees still remain, and as they die they are now being replaced. The fort was finally abandoned in 1871. Today there is a partial reconstruction and a very good museum there.

Capt. Samuel Hensley, who had been with Chiles in 1843 was to lead a pack train west to California. He had hoped to head west from Salt Lake City. However, due to terrible hardships on the salt flats, he was forced to return to Salt Lake City. There he decided to follow a new route north toward Fort Hall that had been opened by Hazen Kimball. Hensley decided to follow it north for about eighty miles and then to head west to meet the well-established California Trail. In crossing this section they encountered a creek, which still bears the name given it—Deep Creek. The route joined the main trail near City of Rocks. This route by Hensley

came to be called the Salt Lake Road, the Salt Lake Cutoff, or Deep Creek Cutoff.

A group of Mormons led by Samuel Thompson decided to return to Salt Lake from California. They had been told that the Truckee River route was very hard and too dangerous to travel so they decided to find a new route. They left near present-day Placerville on July 17. Their company included seventeen wagons, forty-five men and one woman. The route they pioneered has come to be called the Carson route. Tragedy Spring was one of their camping grounds where three of their scouts were killed by Indians, and it retains that name today. Further along the route the Hope Valley was also named by them. They picked up a branch of the Carson River and followed it down the eastern side of the Sierra Nevada, and then cut north over to the Truckee route near the Forty-Mile Desert. Then they continued east over the established trail exchanging information about their new trail with westward traveling emigrants. When they came to Steeple Rock (Twin Sisters) near City of Rocks they turned off to follow Hensley's new route—he had met and told them about it—and they arrived in Salt Lake City on September 20.

Joseph Chiles's company of forty-eight wagons was the largest of the California-bound emigrants. It had followed the trail to Fort Hall and then down the Raft and Humboldt. There they also met the Mormons and were told of the new route. When Chiles came to the Humboldt Sink he turned south along the western side of the Carson Sink and picked up the Carson River, and then followed it until it met the route established by the Mormons. This new sixty-mile section of Chiles's soon became a major portion of the Carson route. Two other companies led by Clyman and Cornwall also used the new Carson route.

Peter Lassen headed east hoping to bring emigrants back over a route that would end near his ranch. He planned to leave the existing California Trail at what is now Lassen Meadows and then follow the Applegate Trail toward Oregon. He hoped he would find a route that would take him west toward his ranch but he ran into problems. He returned with a wagon company, and they turned off on the Applegate Trail as planned, but he could not discover the route he had hoped to find. He traveled further along the Applegate Trail and finally turned off south near Goose Lake. Within a couple weeks they were in trouble and at one time members of the company even threatened to hang him. Fortunately, two large wagon companies coming from Oregon found the tracks where he turned off the Applegate Trail, and they followed them. One was led by gold hungry Peter Burnett. They caught up with Lassen, and with their added strength they were able to cut a new route to Lassen's ranch.

The Lassen Route as it was now called was the third major route to California. However, it was 200 miles longer than the Carson or Truckee routes, given Sacramento as the most common destination. Forty-niners who used this route were misled about claims that it was a cut-off.

1849

This was the year of the gold rush and the forty-niner or argonauts. The California Trail was full of people in wagon companies and pack trains. The trail would have to accommodate about fifty times the number of the people and animals than it had in the previous year. In this year the makeup of the emigrant also changed. Almost all of the emigrants were males off to the diggings or for adventure. And this was also true for the oceangoing argonauts. It was also the first year for a commercial venture to take emigrants to California. Messrs. Allen and Turner had their Pioneer Line. For two hundred dollars they would take about one hundred twenty people west. Poor planning caused problems and hardship all along the way for them. However, this did not stop commercial ventures, and in following years others tried them.

Joseph Ware's guidebook, *The Emigrants' Guide to California*, was published and became popular with many of the forty-niners. He had never been over the trail but compiled it from reports of others—including Frémont and Sublette. He changed the name of the Greenwood Cutoff to the Sublette Cutoff and also recorded the wrong mileage for the crossing of the desert section of it, making it shorter than it really was. Many an emigrant was very unhappy when they found out and very dry at the same time. He made other errors when describing conditions along the Humboldt Valley and sink, calling these areas "rich and beautifully clothed with blue grass." (See a small section of the *Emigrants' Guide to California* in the section on maps and guidebooks.)

On July 19 Benoni M. Hudspeth and John J. Myers broke off from the main trail to Fort Hall just west of Soda Springs near where the Bartleson's party had in 1841. But instead of turning south with the Bear River they headed directly west to meet the California Trail later. By doing so they hoped to cut off the loop north to Fort Hall and thereby save both mileage and time. On July 24 they did come to the main California Trail again. Many of the wagons following behind them saw the wagon tracks turn off the main road to Fort Hall and followed them—almost like "the blind leading the blind." Farnham noted on July 20 that the cutoff "now looks like an old road of a great deal of travel." The road to Fort Hall was used less and less by the California emigrants. Yet, Goldsborough Bruff, captain of the Washington City and California Mining Association wagon train, followed the Fort Hall road and felt that the cutoff really saved little or no time or mileage.

The patterns of usage of the various routes shifted in 1849. West of South Pass the route selected by early emigrants was the Salt Lake Road by way of Fort Bridger. Most of the emigrants that came during the middle of the emigration selected the Sublette Cutoff, and those near the end decided to go by way of Fort Bridger. Out in the Great Basin along the Humboldt River a similar pattern developed. The Carson route seemed to be the most popular with the early emigrants while the Truckee route was selected by those during the middle period. Then on August 11 Milton McGee led his wagon company and turned off at Lassen's Meadow and headed up the Applegate or Lassen route. Again those behind started to follow possibly thinking it was the main route. Even Myers and Hudspeth followed. By the time they discovered what they had done it was too difficult to turn back. On September

19, even Bruff followed. The last emigrants arrived at Lassen's ranch on November 26. Perhaps these shifts were beneficial. If all the emigrants had tried to take the same route the grass and game would have been much less, and the terrible hardships that did exist would only have been made worse.

A state constitutional convention was held and ratified by the voters. A legislature was chosen and Peter Burnett was elected the first governor of California under the constitution on November 13.

1850

Travel along the California Trail doubled that of 1849 with nearly 45,000 emigrants taking the trail. Horses became more popular with the emigrants. Few emigrants would take the Truckee route or the Lassen route, which was now called the "Greenhorn Cutoff." Most emigrants used the Carson route. In this year the emigrants faced even greater hardships than the previous year. Cholera was bad again and took as high a toll as it had in 1849, but the weather conditions were worse and again the increase in usage of the trail took its toll.

California entered the Union as a free state on September 9. Its entrance was made possible by the Compromise of 1850 which balanced the interests of the proslavery groups with those of the antislavery groups. In return for California's entrance as a free state the Fugitive Slave Act was passed, and the Utah and New Mexico territories were organized with the slavery issue to be decided by the residents later.

A trading post sometimes referred to as "Ragtown" was set up on the Carson route after the trail crossed the desert, and further west along the route the Mormon Station had been constructed and then in 1851 it was relocated about a mile south of its original location. Both these trading posts had the effect of making the trek easier although prices were certainly not very modest as many an emigrant complained.

All along the trail improvements were being noted by emigrants, and this trend would increase with each year, new ferries, new bridges, and blacksmith shops sprouting up here and there along the trail. Each year the physical condition of the trail

improved.

1851

Fewer people used the California Trail this year but authorities differ on the number. Historian Merrill Mattes, for example, estimates 5,000-10,000. By now some of the glitter had faded from the gold rush, and emigrants had heard of the terrible hardships along the trail in 1850. Besides, there was Oregon where land was easier to get, and it seemed easier to travel there.

A short but new route was opened at Scotts Bluff through Mitchell Pass. Prior to this the emigrants bypassed the area by going through Robidoux Pass. Today the Oregon Trail Museum is located in Mitchell Pass, and you can walk along the route that was used by so many emigrants and wagons on their way west.

Another branch of the trail was opened by Jim Beckwourth. It turned off the Truckee route north through Beckwourth Pass.

In September the Treaty of Horse Creek or what has sometimes been called the First Ft. Laramie Treaty was signed with the Indians of the Great Plains. The territory was divided into specific tribal grounds, and the U.S. government agreed to provide the Indians with supplies for the next fifty years; the Indians were then to allow the emigrants to pass through their lands unharmed. The peace that this was to ensure did not last very long. Almost immediately some people wanted it changed, and Congress reduced the number of years the Indians were to receive supplies.

1852

This was a banner year for trail travel to California. It was even larger than in 1850. It is estimated that over fifty thousand emigrants including families again traveled over the trails with large herds of cattle and sheep totaling about one hundred thousand. The improvements along the trail were now having their impact. Whereas in 1846 the trip had taken 136 days by ox wagon, this year the fastest made it in 85 days and a mule team did it in 72 days. Unfortunately, cholera was also back on the trail as it had been in 1849 and 1850 and deaths were high.

The Nobles's Road or Nobles' Road was

opened. William H. Nobles took the Lassen route to the Black Rock Desert and then headed west across it and along the Smoke Creek Desert. He then crossed the mountains and headed for Shasta City. This was the type of thing Lassen had hoped to do earlier. The first wagon company consisted of twenty-six people. This would become a popular route during later years.

Another split in the trail developed on the Carson route. This was called the Johnson's Cutoff. It headed off west to the south shore of Lake Tahoe and then to Placerville. This section replaced part of the section pioneered by the Mormons and became the main route for the next ten years. Today U.S. Highway 50 follows the general route.

The Sonora Road was opened. It was another of the splinter routes that broke off the Carson route. It went south to the Walker River and then followed it up and over the mountains to Sonora. This was similar to the route taken by the Bartleson party in 1841. In 1853 this route was heavily used.

Back along the trail just west of South Pass some small cutoffs were also being developed. These cutoffs first followed the trail toward Fort Bridger but turned west near the Green River and later joined the main Sublette Cutoff. They were the Kinney and Slate Creek cutoffs. In a year or so they would be joined by another parallel road the Baker-Davis Road. These became more popular than the main Sublette Cutoff because they cut out the long dry desert crossing of Sublettes Flats.

1853

In 1853 the migration dropped again. However, it was still about twenty thousand emigrants with one hundred fifty thousand head of cattle and sheep.

Another splinter route developed off the Applegate Trail near Clear Lake by the Oregon border. This was the Yreka Road, which took emigrants to northern California and the town of Yreka.

1854

Trouble with Indians increased along the eastern half of the trail in the Platte River Valley. The incident that precipitated the trouble involved a lame cow and an emigrant. The cow wandered off into an Indian village. Instead of trying to obtain the cow back the emigrant continued on to Fort Laramie to get help from the U.S. Army. Lieutenant Grattan, a cannon, and twenty-nine others under his command returned to get the cow. By that time the Indians had already dined on the cow and not much was left. Grattan wanted the Indian responsible for killing the cow. The Indians were willing to give the emigrant a horse in place of the cow, but they were not willing to give up the Indian. Grattan fired the cannon at the village and fighting erupted. When it was over the Brule Chief Bear was dead along with other Indians and Lieutenant Grattan and all of his command save one soldier who escaped to tell of the "massacre." Unfortunately, he died of his wounds two days later. Indians, emigrants, and the army were now at odds and raiding increased for the next couple years.

1855

Travel along the California Trail continued to drop off. This year it was back to the pre-gold rush level and not until 1859 would it almost get back to the 1849 level.

1856

Another splinter developed at the end of the trail. The Big Trees route was opened. It split off the Carson route east of Carson Pass and headed toward Stockton. It was devised by the businessmen of Stockton to divert the emigrant traffic for their own benefit. Improvements were made on the route, and the worst crossings were eliminated by eight bridges with the main bridge being fourteen feet wide and seventy-five feet long. The town even sent out representatives to tell the emigrants of the new road with all its improvements and of all the troubles encountered on the old road.

1857

While the California Trail remained in use traffic was still light. Improvements and additional new routes into California were being developed. Some of them used parts of the California Trail and others bypassed parts of the old routes altogether.

The U.S. Congress appropriated $300,000

for improvements on what was officially referred to as the Fort Kearny, South Pass, Honey Lake Wagon Road, but commonly called the California Trail at least as far as the Lassen Cut-off. Besides improving the grades and crossings, they built reservoirs at places such as Rabbit Hole Spring and Antelope Spring in Nevada, which greatly reduced hardships there.

1858

The Butterfield Stage Line opened. Stage service started at Tipton, Missouri, and then followed the southern route through Texas, New Mexico, Arizona, and then into California.

Fort Bridger was rebuilt by the U.S. Army. It served as a military post until 1890. Nothing was left of Jim Bridger's trading post. Today some of the military buildings have been restored, and it is a living museum and state historic site.

Fort Caspar was established at Louis Guinard's trading post and bridge. It was called the Platte Bridge Station and was named Fort Caspar in 1865 after Lt. Caspar Collins who was killed in the vicinity in the line of duty.

Captain Simpson of the topographical engineers developed a new route from the west side of the Salt Lake. It turned south southwest and then almost due west when it crossed the Nevada line to meet the Carson route. Completed in 1859, it soon became popular with the emigrants.

1859

The Lander Road was opened. This was part of the government's improvement plan started in 1857. Frederich Lander started surveying the area near South Pass for a better route. The route he developed cut off east of South Pass near the Burnt Ranch and headed northwest towards Fort Hall thus bypassing the dip to Fort Bridger or the desert crossing of Sublettes Flats. In 1858 work was started on it and it opened in 1859. It soon became widely used by the emigrants of this later period. One estimate for the first year put the emigration at thirteen thousand.

The Central Overland California and Pike's Peak Express was organized. It started at Leavenworth and headed toward Denver and then to Placerville and California. Its route for the most part was different from the established California Trail.

1860

The Pony Express was established. While it did not last very long it did represent the end of the old era and the beginning of the new. The Pony Express incorporated parts of the California Trail. It started in the east at St. Joseph, Missouri, one of the jumping-off places, and ended at Sacramento, the city that grew up at the site of Sutter's Fort. With the completion of the telegraph in 1861, the Pony Express came to an end.

Fort Churchill was constructed on the Carson route to protect both the emigrants and the growing settlements in the area. Today the area is a Nevada State Park.

Two notable events occurred in 1861 and 1869 on the California Trail. In 1861 there was the worst Indian disaster in the history of the California Trail. It happened east of City of Rocks and is sometimes called the Massacre of Almo Creek. It involved about sixty wagons and three hundred emigrants and the Bannock Indians under Chief Pocatello. The company was under seige for more than four days. Only a few emigrants were able to crawl away during the period of seige. One was the guide who made it to Brigham City and returned with help only to find the wagons burned and almost all the emigrants dead save a few. The 1860s saw more trouble between the emigrants, settlers, and Indians all along both the Oregon and California Trails.

The other event was the completion of the transcontinental railroad in 1869. It often is thought to represent the end of the trail emigration era. In many respects that was true, but for many a poor emigrant the trail west was still the cheapest and only way. The railroad, while not following the complete route, did incorporate parts of the California Trail. Thus, even those who took the "Iron Horse" followed in the footsteps of the early emigrants and argonauts. Today much of Interstate 80 follows the general route of the California-Oregon Trail or one of its branches.

Maps - Guides - Diaries - Artists

Maps—Chart of *Apollo*
Clark's Panama Crossing
Sherman's Map of Sutter's Mill and Gold Discovery
Jefferson's Map of the Emigrant Road
Bruff's Map of the Lassen Route

Guidebooks—Hastings
Ware
Willis
Horn

Diaries—Wilkins
Bryarly
Ingalls

About the Artists—Wilkins
Jackson
Bruff

Maps

This is where it all started. Here is a map of the location of Sutter's Mill where gold was discovered by James Marshall on January 24, 1848. It was drawn in July by William Tecumseh Sherman who was only a lieutenant then. Note that North is at the top, but much of the writing is upside down.

This chart shows the 1849 voyage of the ship *Apollo* which lasted about nine months. The trip "around the Horn" was very popular with the forty-niners. The voyage was about 13,000 nautical miles. Each days position was noted on the chart, and its progress or lack of it can be seen.

The map above shows the crossing of the Isthmus of Panama as drawn by George P. Clark in 1850. The route involved boat travel up the Chagres River and then overland by mule to the Pacific and hopefully another ship.

Here are the sections of T.H. Jefferson's *Map of the Emigrant Road* that was published in 1849. There are four sections of the map. The first two cover the eastern half of the route starting at Independence, Missouri, through the South Pass. Section III starts at the South Pass and continues past Fort Bridger and Salt Lake to the Humboldt River. This route came to be called the Hastings Cutoff. Section IV shows the rest of the trail from the Humboldt River into California via the Truckee route.

There has been some question among historians as to the availability of this map for the emigration of 1849. It does seem that Bruff had a copy of it on his journey, but it is also true that his company was one of the last to leave that year. Jefferson had gone to California in 1846 and was originally part of

the Russell Company, which included Bryant, the Reeds, and the Donners. However, when the company broke up near Fort Laramie Jefferson moved ahead. At Fort Bridger he met Hastings and became part of the party that was organized under Hasting's leadership that made it safely to California over the Truckee route. The slower moving Donner group was never able to catch up with Hastings, due to their own problems and poor instruction from Hastings. The fact that Jefferson returned to New York and had the map published in 1849 would seem to indicate that the route was not that unreasonable in spite of the earlier bad publicity from the Donner disaster. The maps were based on his own work and records together with the Frémont-Preuss maps.

PAWNEE INDIANS.

TABLE OF DISTANCES.

	Miles
From INDEPENDENCE MO. to KANSAS RIVER	95
KANSAS RIVER to NEBRASKA RIVER	217
NEBRASKA R. to SCOTTS BLUFF	353
SCOTTS B. to FORT LARAMIE	56
F. LARAMIE to ROCK INDEPENDENCE	156
R. INDEPENDENCE to SOUTH PASS (culminating ridge)	98
S. PASS. to FORT BRIDGER	111
F. BRIDGER to GREAT SALT LAKE (Utah River)	118½
G. S. LAKE to VALLEY OF FOUNTAINS	243
V. OF FOUNTAINS to MARY RIVER	118½
MARY R. to SINK OF MARY R.	227
SINK OF M.R. to TRUCKEY PASS (summit of Californian Mts)	116¾
TRUCKEY P. to FIRST SETTLEMENT IN CALIFORNIA (Johnsons)	83½
JOHNSON'S to FORT SUTTER	33½
F. SUTTER to ST. FRANCISCO	201¼
TOTAL from INDEPENDENCE to ST. FRANCISCO	2139

Longitude West from Greenwich.

24

MAP

of the

EMIGRANT ROAD

from

Independence Mo. to St. Francisco

CALIFORNIA

by

T. H. Jefferson.

Entered according to act of Congress in the year 1849 by T.H. Jefferson in the clerks office of the district court of the southern district of New York.

PART I.

New York published by the Author 1849.

This map is in four parts and represents the emigrant road from Independence Mo. by the South Pass of the Rocky Mountains to California. The Author was one of a party of emigrants who travelled the road with waggons in 1846. All the streams of water and springs upon the road are delineated, also daily distances, courses and camps made by the party.

EXPLICATION ⚊ Denotes camping places. Figures between the distance in miles. ‒‒‒‒‒ The road travelled The road travelled by some.

KAW INDIANS.

KANZAS RIVER

Santa Fe Road

INDIAN TERRITORY.

MISSOURI

Road to St. Joseph

MAP OF THE EMIGRANT ROAD

from

Independence Mo. to St. Francisco

CALIFORNIA

by

T. H. Jefferson.

PART II.

Copy right secured.

ARAPAHO INDIANS

43°

42°

41°

40°

Fort Hall

Snake River

Oregon Road

Road from Fort Hall to California & Oregon

SHOSHONE INDIANS

BONARK INDIANS

GREAT SALT LAKE

Latitude North.

VALLEY OF FOUNTAINS

DESERT OF UTARIAH

The fearful long drive 55 Miles no grass nor water

Long Drive

35 Miles

Warm Spring

Bonark Mts

115°

114°

113°

Longitude West from Green

MAP OF THE EMIGRANT ROAD

from

Independence Mo. to St. Francisco

CALIFORNIA

by

T. H. Jefferson.

PART III.

Copy right secured.

GOLD
REGION

CALIFORNIA MOUNTAINS

PACIFIC

OCEAN.

Latitude North.

LAGUNA
LAKE.

FRANC
ISCO BAY

Longitude West f

MAP OF THE EMIGRANT ROAD

from

Independence Mo. to St. Francisco

CALIFORNIA

by

T. H. Jefferson.

PART IV.

Copy right secured.

The last map in this section is the one drawn by Bruff showing Lassen's ranch and his route there. If you look closely you will see the route he took over the Lassen Trail from Lassen's Meadow on the Mary's or Humboldt River. Sutter's Fort would be further south down the Sacramento River off Bruff's map. Also included on it is another trip taken by Bruff in the area in 1850. Later Bruff also produced a map of the whole route to California.

Guidebooks

By the end of the 1840s and the early 1850s the emigrants had a much better idea of where they were going and stood a much better chance of getting there. The earliest emigrants had no guidebooks and knew only vaguely where they were. They largely depended on the use of guides or pilots who were usually mountain men, such as, Walker, Bridger, Harris, and Greenwood. The knowledge of the area that these men had was important, but so were their skills at survival because often they had to lead emigrants to lands they themselves had never explored. By the mid-1840s there were enough emigrants themselves who had been over the trails that they began to act as guides or write guidebooks based on their journals. Large sections of the trails were now becoming easier to identify because they had become well worn. This was especially true of the section where the Oregon and California trails coincided.

Guidebooks went through a type of evolution. The earliest, such as Hastings's, didn't tell much about the specifics of the route but provided more psychological support and encouragement. They soon became more specific concerning the routes and by the time of Ware's guidebooks frequently included an overall map of the route. By the early 1850s the better guidebooks such as Horn's used a milepost approach that had been perfected earlier by Clayton in his guide for the Mormons. Also most of the new guidebooks now included one or more of the new cutoffs that had been developed, such as the Hudspeth, Salt Lake, or Sublette, and bypassed the older main routes by Fort Hall or Fort Bridger.

There were a number of guidebooks that played an important role in the westward movement of the emigrants to California. Some of the better known ones today are those written by Hastings, Ware, Clayton, Horn, Child, and Marcy. Another not so well-known today, but well-known to the forty-niners was the small handwritten Willis guide. Portions of some of the above guides will be examined and discussed

briefly, and the small Willis one is included in this volume in its entirety.

Probably the best known early guide is Lansford Hastings's *The Emigrants' Guide to Oregon and California*. It was written in 1844 and printed in 1845. Hastings had gone to Oregon in 1842, moved down to California, and finally returned to the States to encourage more emigrants to go to California. His guide was one of the few available for the earlier emigrants, and it is the one associated with the Donner disaster of 1846. The guide was comprised of fifteen chapters with just over 150 pages. It had, however, only one chapter nine pages long devoted to all the routes to California from Canada to the Horn including a proposed new cutoff, which became known as the Hastings Cutoff. (See Jefferson map.) Most of the guide described what was to be found in Oregon and California. One chapter was devoted to preparations and what to bring—this was probably the most useful of all.

The following quotations are from chapter 14, which was concerned with the different available routes to travel to California and Oregon. First, Hastings described the Oregon Trail west from Fort Hall:

> From this fort, those who go to Oregon, continue down Lewis' river, fifteen days, to Fort Wallawalla; and thence down the Columbia, ten days, to the lower settlements in Oregon.
>
> From Fort Hall to the Pacific, by the Oregon route, a distance of about eight hundred miles, there is but one continued succession of high mountains, stupendous cliffs, and deep, frightful caverns, with an occasional limited valley.
>
> This portion of the Oregon route, from Fort Hall to the Pacific, has always been considered, wholly impassable for wagons, or any other vehicles; yet, it is said, that the emigrants of 1843 succeeded in getting their wagons entirely down to the Wallammette settlement. This they may have done, but I am confident, from my own experience, that each wagon must have cost the owner of it more time and labor, than five wagon are worth, even in Oregon.

Certainly this was not an encouraging description.

Then he described the accepted or old route to California,

> Those who go to California, travel from Ft. Hall, west southwest about fifteen days, to the northern pass, in the California mountains; thence, three days, to the Sacramento; and, thence, seven days, down the Sacramento, to the bay of St. Francisco, in California.

Sounds pretty easy, doesn't it?

Finally he described the geography of both the old and newly proposed routes:

> The California route, from Ft. Hall to the Sacramento river, lies through alternate plains, prairies and valleys, and over hills amid lofty mountains; thence, down the great valley of the Sacramento, to the bay of St. Francisco, a distance from Ft. Hall, of nine hundred miles. The Indians are, in many places, very numerous; yet they are extremely timid, and entirely inoffensive. Wagons can be as readily taken from Ft. Hall to the bay of St. Francisco, as they can, from the States to Ft. Hall; and, in fact, the latter part of the route, is found much more eligible for a wagon, than the former. The most direct route, for the California emigrants, would be to leave the Oregon route, about two hundred miles east from Ft. Hall; thence bearing west southwest, to Salt Lake; and thence continuing down to the bay of St. Francisco, by the route just described.

It's easy to see how people reading this would head for California. It seemed like only a few easy weeks away by wagon from either Fort Bridger and the new cutoff or from Fort Hall if you took the old route. It even implied that the trip was easier once past the forts. For those emigrants that believed him they soon learned that he was mistaken. It seemed he was wrong about almost everything from the Indians to the timing and ease of travel over the "lofty mountains." For many of the Donner party they learned too late. Virginia Reed, one of the young survivors, learned her lesson well and put it best, "Never take no cut ofs and hury along as fast as you can."

Joseph Ware's *The Emigrants' Guide to California* was available to the forty-niners and was a fairly popular one, but while better than Hastings's it was still fairly general for the section of the trail that was exclusively the California section, as can be seen in the following:

> In its course from the Raft river, the road takes a south-western direction, and follows the trail across the dividing ridge to the head of Humboldt or Mary's river, distant one hundred and seventy miles. For two days you travel along the Raft river; camps good. The road over this distance resembles the country west of the South Pass in the Rocky Mountains for the same distance. There are places in which great care is required, and some difficulty may be experienced in consequence of the unevenness of the road in passing over the dividing ridges of the mountains. On the RATTLESNAKE RIVER you can find good camps; there are plenty of good springs also. The prevailing plant is wild sage, which, in some places, will continue to be your dependence for fuel, though there is some good timber.
>
> We would earnestly advise you to oppose any experiments in your party, in leaving the regular route of travel to try roads said to be shorter. You will get to California in good season if you keep straight ahead. If not, you may lose a month or so of time, and experience the fate of the Donner's party. By trying a new road they lost nearly sixty days, and were overtaken by the snow, and spent the winter in the mountains, where nearly forty of them perished. Lose no time foolishly on the road, that can be spent with profit to yourself and teams. You strike the HUMBOLDT RIVER at its head, from thence your course is down its valley for three hundred miles. It is the principal river of the great basin.

There were two guidebooks authored by Mormons. Ira Willis's *Best Guide to the Gold Mines 816 miles* was handwritten. He had gone to California with the Mormon Battalion in 1846 and was nearby when gold was discovered at Sutter's, and even worked at the mill. Returning to Salt Lake with the Mormon group that pioneered the Carson route in 1848, they took the new cutoff back to Salt Lake, which had been pioneered by Hensley earlier that year. This route was the one described in his guide. It was the only guide readily available to the forty-niners that really described a solid and traveled route to California. It seems that both James Wilkins and J. Goldsborough Bruff had copies, which they used.

The other Mormon guide was written by William Clayton. His guide was much more specific and accurate, including a milepost approach and detailed information about water crossings, landmarks, obstacles and camping sites. It became the model for later guidebooks of the 1850s. Clayton's guide covered the route to Salt Lake, and Willis's

---

Best Guide

to the

GOLD MINES

816 miles

by

IRA J. WILLIS

G. S. L. City

---

(2)

Thence to the Old Road near .	the Steeple Rocks,	6.
"	to Goose Creek over a hill	10.
		192.
Several camping places from the		
Steeple Rocks to Goose Creek.		
"	up Goose Creek, good camping.	22.
"	to the Hot Spring Valley	13.
"	" " 2nd Spring (good camp[)]	5.
"	through the Valley	32.
Found good camping places,		
none of them are more than 10 miles apart		
"	to a Branch of Mary's River	
	good camping	8.
"	through a kanyon crossing	
	the Branch 9 times, camping	8.
"	to Mary's River good camping	
	all along	19.
		299.
"	to Martins Fork of Mary's River	
	good camping all along	60.
		. 359.

Way Bill of distances, camping place, rivers, hot springs etc on the Route from G. S. L. to

		Miles
	the GOLD MINES	
To Bear River, crossing the Weber		
4 miles this side of Capt Brown's		
Roadometer Measure		84.
(Good camping at short distances[)]		
Thence to Malad or Mud Creek		3.
"	" the 1st Warm Spring	6.
"	" " 2nd do camping	14.
"	" " Spring in the Mts. good camping	12.
"	down deep Creek cross at the Bend	6.
"	" " " " good camping	6.
"	to Springs in the plains poor "	10.
"	" Cajiers [or Cajius] Creek good camping	
	at several places in sight on left	26.
"	up Cajiers [or Cajius] Creek, good camping	9.
		176.

---

(3)

Thence over a hill through a kanyon		
to where you strike Mary's River again		20.
	(good camping & good in the kanyon.[)]	
Then to a pass in the hills where you		
	cross the River twice good camping	
	all along	72.
"	" the next crossing of Mary's River	
	good camping all along	46.
"	over a drive without grass or water	14
"	to the lower crossing of Mary's River	
	(good camping[)]	14.
"	to the lower camping place on the	
	River, grass-scarce	26.
"	to a Slough, poor camping grass scarce	15.
"	" the Sink of Mary's River .	
	grass & wood scarce	20.
The best water here is in a slough .		586

that passes through a bend & a narrow Bluff. Here also you may find from Salt Lake to California. Compared to Clayton's guide the Willis version was a Spartan edition, but it was better than anything else and was well received. The originals were handwritten and one is currently in the possession of the National Park Service, Yosemite National Park, California, who graciously allowed reproduction from pages of the typeset version.

It seemed that every year new guidebooks were being prepared and generally they were getting better. A few pages covering about one hundred sixty miles from *Horn's Overland Guide* (1852) are included courtesy of the Everett D. Graff Collection, The Newberry Library, Chicago. Horn's guide included the Hudspeth Cutoff on the California Trail. In order to compare it with Hastings's and Ware's start at "West Branch, Raft River." This is where the Hudspeth Cutoff joined the main trail coming down form Fort Hall and the Snake River. Follow it through "Pyramid Circle" (City of Rocks) where the Salt Lake Road joined the main California Trail through "Thousand Springs Valley" and finally to the Humboldt or Mary's River. For a comparison, the equivalent section in the Willis guide is from Steeple Rock through Hot Spring Valley to Mary's River. This same section was also covered in the Hastings's and Ware's excerpts, but as can be seen they were so general that they were of little help for the emigrants. Additionally, both the Willis and the Horn guides used the same general Carson route to cross the Sierra Nevada into California. However, by Horn's time the Carson route had changed some. His guidebook provided added detail, and emigrants felt much more confident with something like this in their hands.

Notable Places, Objects, and Remarks.

EAST BRANCH, RAFT RIVER :   12 1171
—25 feet wide; 3 feet deep. The
banks are remarkably soft, and very
bad crossing; a pretty good place to
camp, though but little fuel.

MIDDLE BRANCH, RAFT RIVER :   2 1173
—20 feet wide; 3 feet deep. This, like
the first branch, is very bad crossing,
and about it are many low places, with
good grass.

WEST BRANCH, RAFT RIVER :   5 1178
—25 feet wide; 3 feet deep. A swift
current and gravel bottom, and though
deep, is pretty good crossing; some
willows and grass; here is also the
junction of the Fort Hall and California roads.

SWIFT WATER :   5 1183
—12 feet wide. Water and crossing
good, but few inducements for camping; now cross several branches to

FORD No. 2, W. BRANCH, RAFT RIVER :   3 1186
—2 feet deep. The banks are somewhat soft, but not bad crossing; the
roads are now pretty good to a

Notable Places, Objects, and Remarks.

SMALL BRANCH :   6 1192
—It affords some good water, but cannot be depended on.

ROCK CREEK :   4 1196
—10 feet wide. About one mile before
you reach this you will observe an
old road turning west across the mountain.

SMALL CREEK :   2 1198
—Good water, and early in the season,
good grass.

WHITE CREEK :   2 1200
—20 feet wide. Be cautious about
turning your stock loose here, as there
are several alkali springs to the right
of the road; the old road keeps south
in the valley; the present one passes
over the hills to

CEDAR CREEK :   3 1203
—8 feet wide. Here we find good water, grass, and fuel, and a good place
to camp; you then drive immediately
into

Notable Places, Objects, and Remarks.

PYRAMID CIRCLE:*　　　　　　　　　5　1208
—And pass through it.

JUNCTION GREAT SALT LAKE AND CALI-
FORNIA ROADS:　　　　　　　　　1　1209
—This is just at the west end of Pyramid Circle, and affords some grass and
fuel, but no water.

SMALL CREEK:　　　　　　　　　　3　1212
—This is the second creek from the
junction; good water, and some fuel
and grass; flat roads.

FLINT SPRINGS AND BRANCH:　　　　4　1216
—In reaching this place you cross a
small creek, about two miles from it;
at this spring and branch you have
good water, and advantages for camping.

* Pyramid Circle is a delightful place. It is 5 miles long, and about
3 miles wide, level within the walls around, and studded throughout
with numerous tall white and green stones, from 60 to 150 feet high,
and 10 to 20 feet in diameter at the foot—some of them running
almost to a point at the top. It is surrounded by mountains which
are covered with pine and cedar trees, and is altogether a beautiful
and picturesque scene. Upon these stones are written, painted, and
engraved, the names of many visitors, with the dates. This circle is
entirely surrounded by the mountains, except an inlet at the east
end of about 50 yards, and an outlet at the west end of about 20
yards.

Notable Places, Objects, and Remarks.

STEEP CREEK:　　　　　　　　　　2　1218
—Just before reaching it you have some
hills and a rough road; down the hill
to the right of the road is some grass
and timber, and a good place to
camp.

OLD ROAD:　　　　　　　　　　　3　1221
—Here on a hill an old road leads to
the right; the road is now hilly and
very rough to

BRANCH OF GOOSE CREEK:　　　　1　1222
—10 feet wide. Some grass and fuel,
and good water.

GOOSE CREEK:　　　　　　　　　3　1225
—25 feet wide; 3 feet deep. The valley of this creek furnishes many good
camping places, and much good grass.

SMALL CREEK:　　　　　　　　　6　1231
—It is not wide, but very deep, with
soft banks.

RECORD BLUFF, to the left:　　　10　1241
—It is a sandstone, upon which is written the names of thousands of travelers; Good Creek is just to the right;
good camping.

Notable Places, Objects, and Remarks.

CAÑON, east end: 4 1245
—The road is quite rough up this *cañon*
along a branch of Goose Creek, to a

STONY HILL: 5 1250
—This hill, though rough and rocky, is
easily ascended.

THOUSAND SPRINGS VALLEY: 9 1259
—Here we find several small streams of
warm water, and some mineral water,
but little that is good to use.

SMALL CREEK: 13 1272
—10 feet wide; 2 feet deep. A good
place to camp; wild sage for fuel,
and tolerable good water, while you
find the best of grass.

HOPE SPRINGS: 24 1296
—You will find considerable branch
water all along before you come to
this spring, but it contains the very
best of water; you will now go south
to the mouth of a

CAÑON: 1 1297
—Where you will find some grass, and
a good place to camp.

Notable Places, Objects, and Remarks.

CAÑON CREEK: 9 1306
—6 feet wide. Good water, but no
grass; you will pass over a rough
road for some distance to

DECEPTION VALLEY: 18 1324
—This valley from the surrounding hills
has the appearance of a beautiful
meadow, but it is all weeds.

DEEP FORK (of Humboldt):   5 1329
—12 feet wide; 4 feet deep. The water is clear, and current swift; some
grass and fuel, and a fair place to
camp.

HUMBOLDT RIVER: 6 1335
—3 rods wide; 5 feet deep. It is very
bad crossing, and within one mile you
cross two other branches of it, which
are also bad; the roads are then good
down the river to

WEST BRANCH, HUMBOLDT RIVER: 23 1358
—4 rods wide; 4 feet deep. A solid
gravel bottom, and good crossing; no
grass.

Diaries

Emigrant diaries came in all sizes and shapes. Each emigrant had their own style. Some like Bruff's (1849) were extremely detailed and illustrated. Others like William Baker's (1852) had only a line or two for each day. Some wrote regularly and others infrequently. Merrill Mattes, eminent historian and authority, suggests that about one out of 250 emigrants kept some form of written record of their journey.

For the historians these diaries are the major source of insights into the trail's history and the emigrants themselves. Yet, no single diary can be considered the definitive one. Conditions on the trail could change in a few days let alone from one year to the next. Different portions of the trail had different characteristics and demands. The organization, planning, and leadership of the wagon company varied but was crucial. Even the character of the particular emigrant had its impact. Each wrote from his/her own perspective, interest, and expectations. Men and women saw things differently. All these factors combined to give each emigrant their own special reaction to the trail and, thus, was reflected in their diary and made it different from other diaries.

Well run companies and poorly run ones shared the trail at the same time and place. Some companies ran out of supplies early, while others still had some to discard or to share with those less fortunate. For some companies it seemed that things were always going wrong, while others had no serious problems. Therefore, one diarist would report a very different impression of the trek west from another. This is not meant to say that they did not have similar experiences, however. Only by examining a variety of diaries can one fully understand the trek west.

The following diary excerpts are from three emigrants: James Wilkins (1849), The Henry E. Huntington Library and Art Gallery, Wakeman Bryarly (1849), Yale University Library; and Eleazar Ingalls (1850), The Newberry Library. The diaries are "typical" in that length, varied greatly and the three short excerpts give insight into what it was like on one major section of the trail. The impact of the different factors and conditions that combined to give them their own personal experience come through clearly to the reader.

By the time the emigrants had reached the Mary's or Humboldt River they had come about sixteen hundred miles, depending on where they began. Yet the worst part of the California Trail still faced them—crossing of the great desert area and then the climb over the Sierra Nevada. If the emigrants hadn't seen it already this is where they got a close look at the "elephant," the symbol of hardships and despair. Come join our three diarists as they leave the Humboldt Sink and head off to cross the Forty-Mile Desert area for either the Truckee (Salmon Trout) River or the Carson River. Emigrants traveling on the Lassen Route had already turned off at the Meadows and had had to contend with the Black Rock Desert. Their experiences were similar to those that will be noted in the following passages. Bryarly would head west for the Truckee, while Ingalls and Wilkins would cut southwest to the Carson.

Notice their comments concerning earlier expectations, the problems of their own wagon company and others, the climatic and physical conditions found and endured on the desert, and its general impact on their own feelings and future expectations. Remember also, the account of Betsey and Ike in the song at the beginning.

Read along and relive their journey as they headed west over the deserts.

Oh, don't you remember Sweet Betsey from
    Pike,
Who cross'd the big mountains with her
    lover Ike,
With two yoke of cattle, a large yellow
    dog,
A tall Shanghai rooster and one spotted
    hog.

They soon reached the desert, where
    Betsey gave out,
And down in the sand she lay rolling
    about;
While Ike, half-distracted, looked on
    with surprise,
Saying, "Betsey, get up, you'll get sand
    in your eyes."

Their wagon broke down with a terrible
    crash,
And out on the prairie rolled all kinds
    of trash;
A few little baby clothes done up with
    care—
'Twas rather suspicious, though all on
    the square

The Shanghai ran off, and their cattle
    all died;
That morning the last piece of bacon was
    fried;
Poor Ike was discouraged, and Betsey got
    mad;
The dog drooped his tail and looked
    wondrously sad.

Sweet Betsey got up in a great deal of
    pain,
Declared she'd go back to Pike County
    again;
But Ike gave a sigh and they fondly
    embraced,
And they travelled along with his arm
    round her waist.

They suddenly stopped on a very high
    hill,
With wonder looked down upon old
    Placerville;
Ike sighed when he said, and he cast his
    eyes down,
"Sweet Betsey, my darling, we've got to
    Hangtown."

Bryarly left St. Joseph, Missouri, on May 10, 1849, and took the Sublette Cutoff. He then went by way of Fort Hall because the Hudspeth Cutoff was not opened when he passed. He reached the sink on August 11 and the Truckee on the thirteenth. On September 11, 1849, he arrived at Johnson's ranch.

SINCE Saturday at 2 o'clock, we traveled 65 miles without *wood* or *water* to last evening [Monday] at 6 o'clock.

Saturday, August 11th.

The morning was fair, beautiful, & pleasant. Early, everything & everybody was in active preparation for a start in the evening. Grass was bundled & packed & stowed in the wagons. Loose mules were packed also, & everyone riding an animal had his fodder behind him. Casks & kegs, gum bags & gun covers, coffee pots & tea kettles, canteens, jugs & bottles, *everything* was filled with water & at 1 o'clock the order to gear up was given & at 2 we bid farewell to the marsh & our numerous friends. The road goes direct across to strike the old road some 5 miles. It was a new one, & made through the sage bushes & of course was not very good, but the old road was as smooth as a table & hard as a rock. It passed over what is in high water part of the sink & consequently there was no vegetation save a few sage bushes, which were upon mounds several feet above the level. Stock of all sorts, horses, mules, oxen & cows were scattered along, having coralled themselves in the arms of fatigue & death. Here for the second time upon our journey we saw the mirage upon these immense white basins. It was a poor example, however, but was very deceiving to those who had never seen anything of the kind before.

Twelve miles upon the old road brought us to the *Sink,* the disideratum of long hoped for weeks. "How far to the Sink?" has been a question *often* asked, & *often* answered, & *often* heard in the last month. This Sink extends over several miles & is generally grown up with rushes & grass. There is immense basins however on all sides, which, in high water, receive the back water. The road keeps in these basins, which extend over *miles & miles* without a vestige of vegetation, but so white & dazzling in the sun as scarcely to be looked at. We rolled by this, the water of which cannot be used by man or beast, [for] 4 miles, & came to some sulphur springs or rather wells. Here we encamped for the night. These wells were dug in a slough, & the water was very like many of our sulphur springs at home. The animals drank it freely & it seemed to do them no harm. In this slough just below the spring were a great number of cattle & mules, which had become mired & were not able to get out & were left. Some of them were still alive. The most obnoxious, hideous gases perfumed our camp all night, arising from the many dead animals around. In the morning some were found laying immediately by us & in the vicinity 30 [others] were adding their scents to the nauseous atmosphere. Our animals were turned to the grass we brought already dried, & they seemed [to] relish it much.

We were *past the Sink*.[5] This is glory enough for one day. I would ask the learned & descriptive Mr. Frémont & the elegant & imaginative Mr. Bryant, where was the beautiful valley, the surpassing lovely valley of Humbolt? Where was the country presenting the most splendid ‘‘agricultural features?’’ Where the splendid grazing, the cottonwood lining the banks of their *beautiful meandering stream*, & everything presenting the most interesting & picturesque appearance of any place they ever saw?

Perhaps Mr. Bryant was speaking ironically of all these most captivating things that he saw, or perhaps he thought it was ‘‘too far out’’ for anyone else but himself to see. If not, I have only to say, ‘‘Oh shame where is thy blush.’’[6]

5. The Sink of the Humboldt, sometimes called Humboldt Lake, in what is now Pershing County, Nevada, was a landmark sought by all emigrants. The ‘‘Sink’’ tended to alter its position in response to the volume of water which the river carried at any given time.

6. Bryant, *What I Saw*, p. 198, spoke of ‘‘numerous . . . varieties’’ of ‘‘heavily seeded and . . . highly sustaining . . . grasses’’ along the Humboldt. Frémont had traversed the Humboldt region on his third expedition, and had described the valley as ‘‘a rich alluvion beautifully covered with blue grass, herd grass, clover, and other nutritious grasses; and its course is marked through the plain by a line of willow and cotton wood trees’’ (*Geographical Memoir upon Upper California* [Washington, 1848], p. 10). Ware, in his *Emigrants' Guide*, p. 32, echoed these descriptions, and stated that the Humboldt valley was ‘‘rich and beautifully clothed with blue grass, herds grass, clover, and other nutritious grasses.’’

These descriptions provoked angry comment from many emigrants. John Caughey gives specimens of this criticism in his edition of Ware's *Emigrants' Guide*, p. 32, n. 49. Among the Forty-niners, Kelly, p. 295, censures Frémont for his description, and McCall, Aug. 16, notes that ‘‘many are bitter in their denunciations of Frémont.’’ A particularly biting comment is a verse which Tiffany, Aug. 5, quotes as coming from the pen of his companion, John Grantham:

‘‘THE HUMBUG’’

‘‘From all the books that we have read
 And all that travellers had said
 We most implicitly believed,
 Nor dreamed that we should be deceived,

That when the mountains we should pass
We'd find on Humboldt fine Blue-grass.
Nay that's not all[;] we learned moreover
That we'd get in the midst of clover.

We have travelled along it several hundred miles, from its commencement from a little pool that you could drink up if thirsty, to its termination in the sink. It is so very crooked in its whole course that I believe it impossible for one to make a *chalk mark* as much so. Frequently I have stood & fished on each side of me in two different parts of the river, the distance around being half a mile or more. It is a *dirty, muddy, sluggish, indolent stream,* with but little grass at the best of times, & as for cottonwood, there is not a switch of it from one end to the other. A friend of mine remarked, it was fit for nothing else but to sink to the ''Lower Regions,'' & the quicker it done it the better. He much preferred calling it Hellboldt River.   [*Distance, 23 miles.*

Sunday, August 12th.

We rolled out at daybreak. The road was firm, hard, level, & smooth. In four miles we came to the forks of the road. Here we found many placards, the most of which advised their friends to take the right. The left was but little travelled in comparison to the right, & we took it.[7] We rolled through the same kind of a basin as yesterday and [at] 10 miles we stopped to breakfast, which was cooked with some pieces of wagons we picked up on the road. We layed by until 2 o'clock having given grass & water to our stock, & again rolled. The road continued the same for several miles, when we left the basin forever, the road then being upon a ridge with a few sage bushes & rocks. We rolled thus 15 miles, which brought us to the Hot Springs.

Seventy dead animals were counted in the last 25 miles. Pieces of wagons also, the irons in particular—the wood part having been burnt—were also strewn along. An ox-

---

Nay, more yet, these scribbling asses
 Told of 'other nutricious grasses'
But great indeed was our surprise
To find it all a pack of lies. . . .

But when we to the Humboldt came
It soon with us lost all its fame
We viewed it as a great outrage
Instead of grass to find wild sage.''

7. Here, Bryarly appears to reverse the facts. At this well-known junction, the left-hand road went to the Carson River, the right-hand road to the Truckee. The Charlestown Company certainly went to the Truckee, as the rest of the journal shows, and therefore must have taken the right. See statement by John Caughey in his edition of Ware, *Emigrants' Guide,* p. 36, n. 55, and Paden, *Wake of the Prairie Schooner,* p. 404.

yoke, [a] wheel & a dead ox; a dead ox, yoke, & wheel; & a wheel, dead ox & a yoke, was the order of the day, every hundred or two yards.

These Hot Springs are one of *The* things upon this earth. The pool is some 25 or 30 yds. in circumference & around it are a great number of springs, some placid & luke warm, others sending off considerable steam & hot water, & others again, bubbling & boiling furiously & scalding. The water when cooled was drinkable, but sulphurish & very salt. There was a great number of kegs & casks, boxes & wagon-beds here, which had been used to cool the water by others. These we filled & after some hours our stock drank it. A piece of meat, held in one [of] the boiling springs, boiled in 20 minutes, perfectly done. By putting the water in your coffee-pot & holding the pot over the bubbling, it would boil in a few minutes. In this way many of us cooked our suppers.

Thousands of dollars worth of property thrown away by the emigration was laying here. Wagons & property of every kind & description, not saying anything of dead animals & those left to die. The machinery of a turning machine that must have cost $6[00] or $700. A steam engine & machinery for coining that could not have cost less than $2[000] or $3000, were also laying here, all sacrificed upon this Jornado. These things they say belonged to the notorious Mr. Finley [?] who also lost 55 cattle out of 80.

[*Distance, 25 miles.*

———

Monday, August 13th.

We started this morning [at] 2 1/2 o'clock. The road was again in a basin & was level, hard, & smooth. Soon after daylight our animals showed evident signs of fagging. Four miles from [the] Hot Spring we came to some sulphur springs. They were very salty & not good, but had been used by others. The sun was most powerful, & the reflection from the shining dirt made it most oppressive. We rolled 12 miles, & having come to where we strike the sand which we have been dreading all the time, we stopped to breakfast. Some of our teams did not get in for some time after the others, they having fagged so much as to fall in the rear.

Here we fed the last of our grass & gave the last of our water. Several wagons were here, the animals having given out & were taken to the river ahead to recruit, which we learned was but 8 miles, but deep sand all the way. Several of us started soon after eating & came on to the river &

luxuriated ourselves & horses with delicious water. The teams started at 1 o'clock but finding they would in all probability give out or at least be a dead strain all the way, they determined to double teams & bring half over & recruit the mules & bring the remainder today. This was accordingly done & seven wagons arrived safe & our animals watered & turned to good grass. Some remained behind with the wagons & water was packed back to them.

This [is] Salmon Trout [Truckee] River. It is a beautiful, clear, swift stream, & the water is delicious. Large cottonwood trees skirt its banks, which gives everything around an air of comfort once more. In approaching it the trees are seen a mile off, & to the parched, famished, & wearied man & beast they are truly "a green spot in the desert." We are safely over *the desert*, however, without losing a single animal, although many are very far gone; but a day or two recruiting, which we think of giving them here, will put them again all right. The water of the Hot Spring which was used freely by both the men & animals affected them most singularly. Two or three hours after drinking, it produced violent strangling to both. The men in particular were very much annoyed also by the most violent pain in the urinary organs. It was truly laughable to see their contortions & twistings after urinating, which they desired to do every hour. The mules also seemed to suffer much, but their symptoms lasted only 10 or 12 hours. Upon examining an old canteen that had had this water in it, with a grass stopper, I discovered the evident fumes of nitre, & upon examination found it [to] contain much, & no doubt these unpleasant symptoms were caused by it. The dead animals were not so numerous today although there was yet sufficient to be very annoying from their perfumes. On the other [Carson] road I am told they are much thicker, more than half of the head emigration having taken that road. [*Distance, 20 miles.*

Tuesday, August 14th.

All night the teams, with loose mules & oxen, were rolling in, causing a general buzz all night. We layed in camp until noon, our mules being in excellent grass. They were then brought up & taken back [on the desert] for our remaining teams, which arrived in camp at 12 o'clock at night. They report many more dead animals upon the road than yesterday. Every train that has arrived has lost one or two upon this last stretch. The weather today was most oppressively hot & we congratulated ourselves we were not on the parched desert.

There is two roads here, one to the left on the same side of the river with a stretch through the sand of 25 miles to water & grass, the other crosses the river & keeps up the river through a kanyon 16 miles & crossing the river many times. From all we have been able to gather, we have determined to cross the river, taking the right hand road. We had today a general inspection of our provisions & find we have only sufficient to last us ten days. This was alarming & our Quartermaster was ordered to look out for more.

Wednesday, August 15th.

All night the starved & famished mules & cattle were rushing through our camp, very much to the annoyance & risk of injury to those sleeping upon the ground. Many teams arrived last night, with the same proportionate loss as those before them. Everyone, without a dissenting voice, cursed the desert, and yet thank God they are over it with their little loss.

The morning was again very hot & we almost dreaded the idea of exposing ourselves to the hot rays of the sun upon the road. Our mules were brought up at 11 o'clock & we again hooked up. We crossed the river & rolled two miles when we came to a sand bluff which was very hard pulling. We passed upon this one mile & a half & nooned, turning our mules across the river to grass, it being the only grass in several miles. Our Quartermaster having made arrangements to obtain some flour & pork from a train behind, the sick wagon was left to bring it when it should arrive. One mile from noon we got off the sand & crossed the river & was soon in the kanyon proper. We passed along this, crossing the river four times in 5 miles. Here night overtook us, & not being able [to] proceed farther, & finding Capt. Smith awaiting us, we pulled out on the side of the road & tied our mules to the wheels, feeding them upon willows & cotton bushes.

Owing to the scarcity of the grass, the Captain determined to keep a camp ahead [of us], & leave [some]one behind at each place to point out the grazing spots, & I [am] to remain behind to take charge of the train. Our herders have been reduced to the ranks, each teamster taking care of his own extra mules, & the other extra ones rode by the men.

A fellow statesman & friend, Mr. Long, having overtaken

us today, invited Mr. Washington to accompany him through [to the diggings], he being upon pack mules & expecting to arrive a week before us. I tendered to him [Mr. Washington] the use of my "Walking Squaw" & he determined to accept & started off an hour before us. By the way, the Hot Spring water acted very singularly upon the "Squaw." Soon after arriving at breakfasting on the morning of the 13th at the beginning of the sand, she was taken with violent pain, as though she had the cholic, & very much to the astonishment of all, she was *confined* & brought forth. This abortion no doubt was caused by the water. We know not her history & consequently cannot tell the pedigree of the little one, or whether she herself had been *imprudent* & *slipt her foot*, but who knows but in this, was lost the race of as fine stock as ever the world saw. "Squaw," with her nation's peculiarity, was as much herself again in half an hour as though nothing had happened, & was hitched to the sick wagon & dragged it through the sand to the river. (The power of endurance of some of these ponies is most astonishing.)

[*Distance, 8 miles.*

Thursday, August 16th.

We had a most unpleasant camp last night, & at daylight we were again upon the road. Yesterday evening it clouded up with heavy black clouds, with rolling, rumbling thunder, accompanied with vivid flashes of lightening. In the course of half an hour we were blessed with a hail storm, with a fine shower of rain. This is the first for 7 weeks & we hailed it with delight. Last night it was cloudy & very dark, with distant thunder, & being [in] the very narrow place in which we were, with high mountains upon each side, and only able to see the sky looking straight up, gave it a most dismal and sepulchral appearance, & daylight was most welcomed. We rolled 3 miles & coming to some grass upon a flat we stopped to breakfast. Here we remained 2 hours & again rolled 5 miles, when we came to better grass & coralled for the day for the purpose of waiting for our provision train, as well as to feed our mules.

We crossed the river today 7 times, making 12 times in all. Some of them were deep & very rocky, with a swift current, so much so as to take some of our mules off their feet. It was amusing to see many of our men riding their mules across. They would do it most cautiously, picking out their way in every step, but in spite of all this, they would frequently fall, sometimes rolling over [on] their sides & coralling them [the riders] most beautifully in the water. Our friend Locke, in particular, was riding "a very high mule" whose legs were "twisted out"—& which landed him most beautifully in Salmon Trout. The current is so strong that a man can but with difficulty walk across, & consequently it is very dangerous to be thrown in. As yet everything has passed in safety & we hope, with care, it will continue to be so. [*Distance, 8 miles.*]

Friday, August 17th.

It rained again last night & a very heavy dew also fell. We started at 6 o'clock & crossed, & recrossed the stream. Eight miles we nooned, crossing in this distance 8 times. Here we had tolerable grass, our Captain having picked it, & left one [of the advance] to point it out to me. We remained here until 2 when we again rolled. In the evening, we rolled 7 miles, crossing the river 4 times, making in all 22. [24.]

The road between the crossings was sandy in some places, rocky in others, & very steep both going up & coming down in others. After 7 miles we emerged in a beautiful, green, velvety valley, which, upon first coming in view, presented a most cheering appearance. We here crossed a slough, the crossing of which was fixed & bridged by our Captain & party ahead. Before this was done, it is said it was almost impassible, each having to be cordelled across. We passed over in safety & encamped in this lovely valley, with blue grass to the horses' knees. We passed today two graves; one had been drowned several days before, the other had died today. We came in sight for the first time of the Sierra Nevada mountains, or rather of the chain. During the day it has been cloudy, with constant rumbling of thunder in the distance. In the morning we had a very nice shower, & several times during the day it gave us a pleasant sprinkle. [*Distance, 15 miles.*]

Wilkins left Weston on May 8, 1849, and traveled via Fort Bridger and the Hudspeth Cutoff. On September 9 he arrived at the sink, traveled over to the Carson, and then to Sutter's Fort and Sacramento by October 16, 1849.

Sunday Sep[r] 9th

Came only about 18 miles since our last encampment to this place, where we have been laying two days, cutting hay. we are now about 15 miles from the sink, and as we have found unexpectedly good grass, we think it better to lay in our supply here for the desert, and recruit our cattle, than to risk going further, for all is uncertainty and rumour about the road in advance. This is the last good water we shall have for 70 miles they say, and we are filling every vessel that will hold it. The great object of dispute amongst us now is which of the two roads we shall take, that we are informed branch [‡] off from the sink over the desert. The old road or what is called Child's road. the reports about them are so contradictory, that we do not know what to do. Provissions are getting very scarce along the road among the emigrants generally. we have as much hard bread and bacon left as is necessary, but our sugar flour vinigar beans dried apples in fact every thing else is gone, and we must see hard times before we reach California. The late barren country we have passed thro' has told hard upon our cattle—and others too, if we may judge by the number of dead [‡] cattle we passed the last 18 miles. We expect to leave here some time to night, and go down to the sink by daybreak so avoid the midday sun, as the reflection from it on the sand makes it intensely hot in the middle of the day, and distresses our cattle very much. Scurvey is becoming very prevalent among the emigrants. we have heard of several deaths with it——

[1]This entry opened with five and a half lines which Wilkins later struck out: "I wish California had sunk into the ocean before I had ever heard of it. here I am alone, having crossed the desert it is true, and got to some good water. but have had nothing to eat all day, my companions scattered, our wagons left behind. that desert has played h—l with us."

Wednesday 12th

[1]We arrived at the sink [‡] late in the night [Sunday, September 9], having found it 25 miles instead of 15, [‡] the

water poisonous, and not a spear of grass. we pushed on near 3 miles further to where some holes had been [‡] dug in the ground, and water strongly impregnated with sulphur had been found. but few of our cattle would touch it, thirsty as they must have been. here we rested 2 or 3 hours till the moon rose, gave them some hay and pushed on into the desert, 45 miles to the next water. we [‡] took the left hand road or Childs cut off, as it is called and traveled till eleven the next day [September 10], when we stopped and fed the oxen and ourselves. Wide plains of sand salt lying thick on the ground in some places, with here and there a few bushes of grease wood. the mirage exists here. lakes of water, appearently but a few miles from us. About one O'clock, the D—— and I rode off to go thro' leaving the wagons to follow. here commenced the great distruction of property. abandoned wagons dead cattle and articles of every discription lay strewed along the road. between that time and dark, that is for the next 16 miles I counted 163 head of dead stock oxen mules and horses, 65 wagons, some of them entire, others more or less demolished, about 70 ox chains, yokes, harness, trunks, axes, and all minor things I did not count, and these only while riding along the road. doubtless there were a great many I did not see. holes had been dug in different places for water, but it was so strongly impregnated with salt, as to be scarcely drinkable. about dusk we came up with the pioneer wagons left on the road, their mules being unable to drag them further. they had taken them out and drove them on to the river to recruit. the passengers those that were able walked on. but there were a great many sick, and unable to walk. these had to stay with nothing but salt water to drink. amongst them a Mr James was expected to die with the scurvey. they like us had nothing left but bread and bacon, and for these they were indebted to the ox teams on the road. three dollars a pint was offered for vinegar. A soft heavy deep sand commenced here, and continued to the river, (about 10 miles,) thro which our horses laboured severely. we sighed for our cattle, and judging from the smell which saluted our nostrils every few minutes, for it was dark they must have lain pretty thick on the ground. here we met Turner going back with a few mules to fetch one of his wagons containing those most severely sick. About 10 O'clock we arrived at the river and found the pioneer passengers asleep around an immense log fire, for here are actually some large cotton wood trees, the first we had seen since leaving the settlements. We toasted a slice of bacon and eat a cracker that we had brought with us, and lay down beside the fire to sleep. I did not rest much it being too cold, but got up and sat by the fire till mornᵍ. At day break [September 11] the Dʳ returned to meet the wagons, which he met about 6 miles back found several of the oxen had given out, so he concluded to leave them for the day and drive on the oxen to water and grass to recruit.——

Thursday 13ᵗʰ

All day yesterday I was alone huntᵍ our boys, without success till evening. I met E P—— he informed me of the condition of things. several of the oxen still back in the desert. I lent him my mule to ride back and fetch them in, and to bring some bed clothes and provisions, and to meet me at the Pioneer herdsmens camp two miles down the river, where they had driven the rest of the cattle for grass, there being none nearer. Thither I went and waited all night but he came not. this mornᵍ early I set off, determined to find some one that would give me a breakfast. I met E P—— coming on my mule. it seems they were unable to get the cattle down last night but gave them some hay they had, and stayed at the upper camp, or where the road first strikes the river, where he told me to go, and I should find some provissions. I accordingly came on, and got some hot water slightly colored with coffee, and hard bread. to night we shall get up the oxen and fetch in the wagons if we can.——⁷

⁷At the close of this entry Wilkins struck out four lines: "I have just sold my mule having 20$ offered for him. as we have got over the worst part of the road and not more than 200 miles to go I thought I had better take it, as he would be a trouble to me after I got there."

Sunday 16ᵗʰ

We only left our campᵍ ground near the Pioneer's last evening, having been detained by fetching in from the desert 6 or 7 miles back an abandonned wagon, which it was said was much lighter than one of ours, and a good wagon. but after it was brought in and examined by the parties interested, it was risolved to take the old one so by shortening her up and cutting two feet off the bed, and otherwise lightening her, it was thought the teem would pull her thro'. All our cattle are much exhasted and reduced in flesh, as well as other peoples'. I pity those families very much and tremble for their safety that are a week or two behind. Mr James of the pioneers died and was buried yesterday, "with a blanket wrapt around him." what a tale of suffering and neglect he could tell, if the dead could speak. Turner offers 500$ to any one that [‡] will fetch in his provision wagons 3 in number and about 16 miles out, but no emigrants have teems enough [‡] to do it. We came 5 or 6 miles last night to better grass. to day we are going to cut hay to take with us, for it is reported we have another desert of 20 miles to cross. at the commencement of the journey that would be thought nothing of, but here it is "*some*." Emmigrants make a great mistake in calculating upon the load getting lighter. the team get weaker just in proportion.

Wednesday 19th Sep^r

The nearer we approach the end of our journey the more tedious and irksome does the journey become. But a fortnight I expect will carry us thro'. "*Patience thou rosy lip^d cherrub.*" We are most of us taking the scurvey, myself amongst the rest. the gums bleed and the skin is becoming discoloured in patches, particularly about the legs. I have eaten nothing but bread lately, rejecting *fried bacon.*— Carson's river [‡] is a small stream of good water about 1 rod wide and 18 inches deep. its margin is marked by a line of cotton woods of large size, lovely to behold to our *desert-weary* eyes, differing from Marys river which has nothing but willows. for 300 miles down its banks I did not see a tree thicker than my wrist. The weather continues hazy, making the hills or mountains on each side difficult to be seen. On monday night we saw a large notice stuck up by side of the road, informing us the 20 or some said 25 mile desert might be avoided by going about 10 miles round. about 8 miles of the road heavy sand, and then fine grass valeys, besides other information. this was put up by a philantropic Kentuckian, who had been in advance and returned. A leading man of our party observed he was a fool for his pains, tho' he profited by the information. We went that road and found the best grass we had seen for several hundred miles. It has been observed on this road that a man may have travelled to Sante fee and Chiwawa, and yet derive no information necessary for a trip to California. Of this I suppose Mr Turner can bear witness. speaking of Turner Mr Garritt of the Planters house Peoria told me that he offered 3000$ to any one that would take his receipts and pay his expenses for this trip, that he had done all that a man could do for the comfort of his passengers, but what can a man do in a desert. he has purchased provissions from the emigrants at an enormous price, that the order passed for reducing every mans baggage to 75 lbs was from a committee of 12 and not from him, that his own private stores that he had laid in to emeliorate the ruggedness of the route, went in the general wreck.   That was the time an Irishman observed when the old Cogniac "*watered the plain.*" Besides the wear and tare both of body and mind that Turner went thro' must have been great. Garett observed he had seen him drop asleep as he stood. With watching thro' the night, as he was in continual fear some of the men would steal his mules, and been harassed during the day, he must have had a hard time of it. Most of the able bodied passengers are leaving some taking it on foot, and some on horseback, so that his loads will be light from this onward. And I think he will get through.——

Ingalls headed west in 1850 from St. Joseph, Missouri, on May 3, 1850. He traveled by way of the Sublette Cutoff. He arrived at the Humboldt Sink on August 4 and reached the Carson River on the sixth. His journey ended August 21, 1850, when he came to "Hangtown" or Placerville.

Eleazar Stillman Ingalls

July 27th. Started at four o'clock, A.M., traveled down the river two miles, then left the river, struck across a desert plain 12 miles to the river; many think this the Great Desert; it is desert enough, but not the Great Desert. This point will be known by a high mountain dividing two valleys. The river runs to the right of this mountain. At noon we had to feed our horses on willows, there being no grass. We got some rushes by swimming the river. We have now got far enough along to begin to have a sight of the Elephant. The river here runs through narrow clay banks like a canal. Passed the grave of a man found in the river; camped at night on a sand bank, put our horses across the river; grass poor. 17 miles.

July 28th. Sunday. Crossed a sand ridge about two miles, and travelled down the bottom about four miles, where we found some grass and camped. Our horses are failing fast. Kit Carson says truly that the Humboldt is the burying ground for horses and oxen. We pass daily great numbers of dead stock at the camping grounds, in the sloughs, and in the river. The river is nothing but horse broth, seasoned with alkali & salt. The appearance of emigrants has sadly changed since we started. Then they were full of life and animation, and the road was enlivened with the song of "I am going to California with my tin pan on my knee." "Oh, California, that's the land for me," but now they crawl along hungry, and spiritless, and if a song is raised at all, it is, "Oh carry me back to Old Virginia, to Old Virginia's shore." Well, they say misery loves company, so we can have some enjoyment after all, for there is plenty of that kind of company. No one seems to know where we are, even those who traveled the route last year, several of whom are along. Last year the road led immediately on the bottom, but this year it is on the sage plains or second level of the river, the bottoms being so swampy that they cannot be crossed. The Mormon guide for this end of the route, is good for nothing. Yesterday was the worst day for dust that we have had. Every body was literally covered with it so that the drivers could not be recognized. 6 miles.

July 29th. Litwiler and Ranaban killed three antelope yesterday. They packed in two of them about eight miles from the mountains. They arrived in camp about 11 o'clock at night. Passed the clay banks, some perpendicular banks on the opposite side of the river about 50 feet high. From this place is a desert, the river running through narrow clay banks, void of vegetation except the Artemesia or wild sage. The road generally follows the plains back from the river, only approaching occasionally for water. We camped about three P.M. and managed to get a little grass for our horses. 15 miles.

July 30th. Started at four A.M.; route similar that of yesterday. We are now in sight of the Pyramid, a lone peak nearly opposite the upper slough of the sink commonly called the meadow. Road touched the river once or twice to-day for water, but no grass, nothing for feed but willows. 16 miles.

July 31st. Started at one o'clock, A.M., struck the river again 10 miles from camp; no grass, only an arid sage desert. From this it is 25 miles to the slough or meadows, and 13 to water, which will be found at some springs in the gully directly opposite the pyramid. We reached the springs about 10 o'clock, A.M., although one of our horses gave out, which delayed us somewhat, and reached the upper end of the slough about noon, where we obtained some rushes and flags for our horses which they devoured greedily after their long fast on willows. The pyramid at a distance resembles an ancient Mexican pyramid, rising by steps. It may be seen for 40 miles up the river, and serves as a beacon, for the slough or meadows. After baiting we continued down the slough about six miles to some passable springs, and to where there is better grass. We found two cities of tents at the slough quite populous. They would do honor to more civilized countries. The road for a few days past has been strewed with dead stock. I counted to-day 120 head of horses, mules and oxen, and got tired of it before night at that. I suppose I passed 50 head more that I did not count. If there is any worse desert ahead than we have found for 70 miles back, I don't know what it may be. I have noticed several dead horses, mules and oxen, by the road side, that had their hams cut out to eat by the starving wretches along the road; for my own part I will eat the lizards which infest the sage bushes, before I will eat the stock that died from the alkali. The destitution has reached its height now. Hundreds are entirely out of provisions, and there are none who have any to spare, and but very few who have enough to carry them into the mines. Often, almost daily, will some poor starved fellow come up to the wagon and pray us in God's name to give or sell him a crust of bread; some of them asserting that they have eaten no food for two, or even three days. Money is no consideration for food here; no one will sell it for money, but we always give enough to prevent starvation, when thus importuned, although we have not over five day's provision on hand, putting our trust in Providence for the issue to ourselves — for so long as there is game in the mountains we will never starve.

To-day is the first since the third day of June, that we have been out of sight of snow for a whole day; it has been excessively hot, the dust rising in clouds; roads bad, owing to the deep sand. 32 miles.

August 1st. Remained camped to-day, preparing hay for crossing the Desert, which commences 20 miles from the slough or meadow. There is an abundance of grass at this point for all the stock that can ever reach here. We have to wade to get it, then cart it to the channel, and boat it across that in a wagon box. A man with his wife came into the camp last night on foot, packing what little property they had left on a single ox, the sole remaining animal of their team; but I was informed of a worse case than this by some packers, who said they passed a man and his wife about 11 miles back who were on foot, toiling through the hot sand, the man carrying the blankets and other necessaries, and his wife carrying their only child in her arms, having lost all their team.

August 2nd. We still remain at the meadows. A team came in yesterday evening from Sacramento, loaded with provisions. They ask for rice $2.50 per lb.; for flour $2.00; bacon $2.00; whiskey $2.00 per pint, and brandy $3.00 per pint. We killed a cow this evening which we had picked up a few days ago at a camping ground, where she had been left on account of lameness. She was not exactly beef, but she was better eating than dead mules and horses by the road side; we divided her up in the train and among the starving people who are about us, only saving a small amount for ourselves, which we jerked and dried.

August 3rd. We are still lying by. About two miles below our camp are some falls in the river, at which point the meadows terminate. There is no more grass from here until we reach Carson River, about 66 miles. — Some of the teams that left us above Fort Kearney came in to-day, entirely destitute of provisions, and had been so for some days, although they had contrived to starve along somehow. We heard of them before they got here, and saved a little beef for them.

August 4th. Sunday. Broke up camp and started again. We had stopped three days to recruit our horses before taking the desert, and although we have taken the utmost pains with them, they are weaker now than when we stopped. My advice to all is not to make any stop at this point, but push on to Carson River, for there is so much alkali in the water and grass here that your stock will not recruit. There is no water for the next 20 miles fit for stock to drink. We lost one horse to-day from watering beside the road, four miles before we got to the sink. He died in thirty minutes after drinking, in the greatest agony. Two others were much injured, so much so, that we could only get them to the sink with the greatest difficulty. Trimble and Sublet also lost one. Beware of shallow water along here. 20 miles.

August 5th. Reached the Sink last night about sunset. This is a basin about 80 rods wide and half a mile long. It is usually the last water found on the Humboldt, or where it loses itself in the sand, hence its name, but this year the water is so high that it runs down several miles further before it entirely sinks. There is no grass here whatever, nothing but desert. We broke up our wagon to-day and made pack saddles, being convinced of the impossibility of getting our wagon across the desert, since the loss of the horse yesterday and the injury to the others. Last night while we were making our supper on coffee and boiled corn, soon after dark, a man came to us and asked for a drink of water. I gave it to him; after drinking he stood looking wistfully at our corn, then asked me if I would take half a dollar for a pint cup full of it. I told him I would not take half a dollar for it, for money was no consideration for food here. He said no more, but turned sorrowfully away, when I stopped him and asked him if he was in distress. He said that he had eaten nothing for two days but a small piece of dried meat which a man gave him. I then told him that I would not take a half dollar for the corn, but that he was welcome to sit down and eat his fill; for although we were nearly out of provisions, we would divide with a man in distress to the last morsel. He stopped the night with us, and took breakfast, and although urged to stop and cross the desert with us to-day, or take some corn with him, he would not do it, but said that he had taxed our hospitality too much already, and left us this morning. His name was Bayell, he belonged in one of the central counties of Illinois, and was a man of standing and influence at home, and a brother of the I.O.O.F. He said he hailed when he came up to our camp, but it was so dark that I did not see his hail, or I should not have put him to the test, to see whether he was really needy or not. Sublet and company, and Williams & Co. left us this morning to cross the desert; we got our pack saddles completed, and took the desert at 2 o'clock, P.M., and traveled all night. Two of our horses gave out, the same that were alkalied, and we left them. About midnight we reached the first wagon road where we found about four acres of wagons left to decay on the desert; this is the first sand ridge; we passed two other wagon yards before morning at similar ridges, besides great numbers along the road, many of them burning. Who will accurately describe this desert at this time? Imagine to yourself a vast plain of sand and clay; the moon riding over you in silent grandeur, just renders visible by her light the distant mountains; the stinted sage, the salt lakes, cheating the thirsty traveler into the belief that water is near; yes, water it is, but poison to the living thing that stops to drink. Train after train drag their tiresome course along, man and beast suffering all the pangs of thirst toil on, feeling, knowing that if the burning sun finds them on the desert in the coming day, their sufferings will be enhanced ten-fold, if worn out with fatigue and thirst they do not faint by the wayside and give up altogether. Burning wagons render still more hideous the solemn march; dead horses line the road, and living ones may be constantly seen, lapping and rolling the empty water casks (which have been cast away) for a drop of water to quench their burning thirst, or standing with drooping heads, waiting for death to relieve them of their tortures, or lying on the sand half buried, unable to rise, yet still trying. The sand hills are reached; then comes a scene of confusion and dismay. Animal after animal drops down. Wagon after wagon is stopped, the strongest animals are taken out of the harness, the most important effects are taken out of the wagon and placed on their backs and all hurry away, leaving behind wagons, property and animals that, too weak to travel, lie and broil in the sun in an agony of thirst until death relieves them of their tortures. The owners hurry on with but one object in view, that of reaching the Carson River before the broiling sun shall reduce them to the same condition. Morning comes, and the light of day presents a scene more horrid than the route of a defeated army; dead stock line the roads, wagons, rifles, tents, clothes, everything but food may be found scattered along the road; here an ox, who standing famished against a wagon bed until nature could do no more, settled back into it and dies; and there a horse kicking out his last gasp in the burning sand, men scattered along the plain and stretched out among the dead stock like corpses, fill out the picture. The desert! you must see it and feel it in an August day, when legions have crossed it before you, to realize it in all its horrors. But heaven save you from the experience.

An incident occurred this evening which shows well of the selfishness of some people on this route. It was soon after dark; we had taken off the packs to rest our horses, and were sitting and lying in the sage bushes beside the road; one of our companions had a few miles back been compelled to leave a horse, which from mistaken feelings of sympathy for the poor animal, he had neglected to kill. While sitting there, a company of packers came along the road, when, although it was so dark that I could not distinguish one animal from another, our friend caught up his rifle, cocked and presented it towards one of them, exclaiming in an angry tone, "Get off that horse, you g———d d—n—d scoundrel, or I'll shoot him down under you." The fellow slid off the horse instantly, when our friend gave him one of the "dog-onit-est" blowings up, as the Missourians say, that one fellow ever got for riding the poor animal after he had given out. It was our friend's horse, who, dark as it was, recognized his faithful animal. The fellow sloped without saying a word in his defence.

August 6th. Morning still finds us dragging our weary steps along on the desert, with nothing near but endless sand hills and beds of clay. Passed Sublett's and Trimbles and Williams's wagons, which they were compelled from loss of stock to leave. Reached the last sand 13 miles from Carson's River, about 10 o'clock, A.M., where we found a water station, and bought some water for our horses at 75 cts. a gallon. We left the pack of one horse here for the station keeper to bring in at night, and the boys went on with the horses, leaving Fuller, who was pretty much done over, and myself, behind. They reached the river about four o'clock, P.M. We were fortunate enough to find some old friends, P. Welch, and T. Ranahan, who had got up a shelter for themselves and oxen, of tents, cloths, and wagon covers, to protect them from the sun. We stayed with them through the heat of the day, and about night started again, but turned off about a mile from the road to visit a small salt lake, where we found a very good spring of fresh water and a sulphur spring. This lake is about three miles from Carson River; its waters are more salt than the most salt brine, and its shores are encrusted with pure salt. Its bed was evidently once the crater of a volcano. We reached the river about 10 o'clock, P.M., but could not find our camp it was so dark, although we found the next day that we had passed directly through it, but the loss of tents, wagons, &c., rendered it impossible to distinguish our comrades who were snoring away, wrapped in their blankets. However, after straggling around until towards midnight, we found the tent of some old esteemed friends, Esq. Hoffman & son, who gave us a hearty welcome and a spare blanket, which, (having already filled ourselves with God's beverage from the Carson River,) was to us a perfect elysian. 46 miles.

Artists

Most of the paintings and drawings that follow in the book are the works of James F. Wilkins, William Henry Jackson, and J. Goldsborough Bruff. In addition there are some that are drawn by other artists and emigrants. The recent photographs that accompany the early ones were taken by the author on his recent trips along the California Trail.

James F. Wilkins joined an ox wagon company and headed for California with the rest of the argonauts during the gold rush of 1849. He had come to the United States about 1836 from England and first set up shop as a painter in New Orleans and later in St. Louis where he established a reputation as a respected portrait painter. He set out April 25, 1849, from St. Louis on his adventure to the gold diggings. He planned his trip with the sole idea of painting scenes along the trail, and then to return as soon as possible to paint his large moving murals or panoramas, which were a popular style at that time. He reached the diggings in October and by December he was on his return voyage. He had made about two hundred watercolor sketches of scenes along the trail. Upon his return he prepared his panorama and toured parts of the United States with it for a few years. Little information is known about him in the years following his tour, and he died on his farm in Illinois in 1888. Most of his paintings and sketches were not signed and over the years his works have often been attributed to other artists. Even the locations of the scenes have sometimes been incorrectly identified in some publications. Of the approximately two hundred sketches he had when he returned only about fifty of them are presently known to exist. All of these are from the first half of the journey up through Soda Springs. None are from the Nevada-California section of the trail.

As a result of the work of the eminent historian John McDermott's research in the 1960s approximately fifty drawings were identified as Wilkins's. However, some books published in the 1970s and even the early 1980s still had them improperly identified. Included in the corresponding photographs are some scenes that are specifically located for the first time in a publication. One of the things noticed about Wilkins's paintings was his tendency to make his paintings more compact. This tendency to squeeze the landscape together may have made it more appealing, but it also had the effect of adding height to his subject. This will be obvious when you compare some of his drawings with the photographs of today. In a similar way he tended to make his mountains pointed even when they weren't. Once these two techniques of his were understood it became much easier to locate most of the specific locations on the California Trail from which his drawings were made. Today his drawings are located at the State Historical Society of Wisconsin.

William Henry Jackson was born in 1843 when the California Trail was just opening. He did not travel on it until 1866 when it was almost past its heyday. Yet, much of the scenery along the trail had not changed much during the twenty some years that had ensued after its opening. Jackson signed on as a bullwacker on an ox freight wagon team and headed west from Nebraska City. Near Ham's Fork he quit his job, but then joined another wagon company and headed down to Salt Lake City. There he joined another company headed to California by way of the Salt Lake-Los Angeles Road, which coincided with part of the Old Spanish Trail. He returned from California in 1867. During his trip he made many sketches that became the basis for his paintings, which were mainly done in the 1930s. He is perhaps best known for his photographic work of the early West, which started in 1869 when he worked for the Union Pacific Railroad. Then in the 1870s he served as the official photographer for the Hayden Survey of the Territories, and he was instrumental in making Yellowstone into the first national park. Some of his early photos and those of others were also used as a basis for his later paintings. Jackson's original trail sketches and many of his paintings are now on exhibit in the Jackson Memorial Room of the Oregon Trail Museum at Scotts Bluff National Monument. Still other Jackson paintings are displayed at Harold Warp's Pioneer Museum at Minden, Nebraska.

J. Goldsborough Bruff was the captain of a wagon company from Ohio called the "Washington City and California Mining Association" that headed west for the California diggings in 1849. He had earlier trained at West Point as a civilian cartographer. His company was comprised of seventeen mule-drawn wagons and sixty-six men. This was typical of the gold rush years as the men went off to make their fortunes while the women remained back home. He kept a diary of his journey, and it is perhaps one of the best and certainly longest of all the ones written by the forty-niners. Not only did he include the typical comments about the trail, the topography, and his experiences, he also included numerous pencil and pen sketches of scenes and events and even information about graves and tombstones along the trail. His sketches were very accurate and became the basis for his later paintings. It seems even he fell into the pattern of other painters and when going from his pen and pad to his brush and canvas he sometimes tended to exaggerate some features making them look even more dramatic than the sketches showed. Probably the largest collections of his works are located in The Huntington Library and at the Beinecke Rare Book and Manuscript Library, Yale University Library. Many copies of the original pen sketches can also be found in his book, *Gold Rush*.

Bruff returned east and went to work for the government and the topographical engineers. He produced one of the early maps showing the way over the Sierra Nevada by the Lassen Road and also two maps showing the complete emigrant trail across the country.

Travel westward now, and see the trail as depicted by the artists, and compare it with the trail today.

All the photographs and drawings in this section have their corresponding sites located on the overall maps of the trail located on pages viii and ix.

Pictorial Journey

Courtesy, Museum of New Mexico #3083 by Ben Wittick

Here is an emigrant train nooning on their way west, and below is a recent Oregon-California Trails Association "wagon train" nooning on a recent expedition on the Sublette Cutoff. Travelers of both periods welcomed any shade during the heat of the day.

One of the early morning tasks on any wagon company was to round up the animals and to yoke up the oxen. Here is Jackson's drawing of it.

Below is a picture of the oxen grazing today at Rock Creek Station. Notice the height of the grass. Unfortunately for most of the emigrants they were never able to find grass this tall along the immediate trail. It had usually been eaten off or trampled on by hundreds and thousands who came before them. At Deer Creek Wilkins wrote on July 2, 1849, that "such a number of cattle had been before us, that it was all eaten off close. it was computed . . . we should have to drive our cattle seven miles to feed." More typical was his statement of the sixth, "had difficulty in finding a scanty supply of grass 2 or 3 miles from the road."

One of the constant complaints of the emigrants was the dust along the trail. It got into everything. Their eyes burned and they coughed trying to breathe. In July 1850, Charles W. Smith wrote: "Our road is very dusty. The dust is so light the least wind raises it. . . . Sometimes the dust is so heavy that we cannot see the wagon immediately ahead of us in the train." Even today modern trains have trouble with the dust and become strung out so they do not eat each others dust.

Water was a major problem along some sections of the trail. Frequently emigrants were forced to dig in the dry riverbeds or ravines hoping to find water. Here is an example of it today at the Dry Sandy. Some of the actual "tanks" dug by the emigrants are still visible there and at other places along the trail.

One other frightening experience for the emigrants was the terrible thunderstorms along the Platte. Jackson drew this one based on his own experience while camped by a Mormon train. Emigrants often noted the rain was so hard their canvas covers and tents were of little real use and everything was soon soaked. Jackson wrote, "The rain beat down so hard it came through the Canvas like a sieve."

Below is a part of the living display of a trail re-enactment at Scotts Bluff that was caught in a thunderstorm.

Death was a constant companion for the emigrants. Some historians estimate that there is a grave for every five hundred feet. Here is the grave of a young woman buried at Emigrant Spring on the Slate Creek Cutoff. The grave, which was in danger of being washed away, was recently excavated and relocated by the Oregon-California Trails Association. The young woman's grave was very elaborate. She appears to have been buried in a coffin made from parts of a wagon box surrounded by stones. Most emigrants were hastily buried often in the trail itself as a protection against desecration by animals or Indians.

Many emigrants encountered different Indians along the way. This Shoshone encampment near the South Pass was photographed by Jackson.

During the early years most encounters were friendly. However, by the 1850s and then the 1860s conditions became much worse, and hostilities became more common. But, in reality accident and then disease, not Indians were the major killers of emigrants along the trail.

This is one of the posters extolling the virtues of both the ship and the voyage by sea to California and the gold fields.

Here is San Francisco harbor literally jammed with vessels. Many of them were abandoned by their crews and left to rot while the crews took off for the gold diggings.

National Park Service

Jackson saw Westport Landing more than twenty years after its development as a trailhead. By then the area had been built up. Here is his vision of what it looked like in its earlier years.

Westport Landing as it appears today. Jackson would have a hard time recognizing it.

This well known drawing of Independence Square shows Independence as many emigrants would have seen it. *Artist Unknown.*

Today the courthouse is much larger, and it is said to contain remnants of the earlier courthouses. As in the past the square is still a hub of activity.

This is a photograph of Spring Park in Independence. The restored cabin is the Brady Cabin one of the oldest structures in Independence. It was moved to this location in the 1970s.

Further up river nearly across from Fort Leavenworth was the town of Weston. Wilkins disembarked here in 1849. This is the Sebus house which was standing when he arrived.

Landing at Weston   May 2 1849

MISSOURI RIVER PACKET ALICE

Wilkins drawing of the landing when he arrived at Weston. Today Weston is a small town, and no longer the hub of activity like it was in 1849 or the early 1850s when it was a jumping-off place.

This photo shows the same corner of town visible in Wilkins' drawing. The building to the left is on the bank which led to the river during Wilkins time. Today the river channel has shifted about two miles to the west.

Wilkins passed Fort Leavenworth aboard a steamboat on his way to Weston on the east side of the river about May 1, 1849 and made this drawwing of its landing area. By then the fort was already twenty-two years old.

The landing area at Fort Leavenworth today. Note the deep swale going up the hill in the center. That is the beginning of the trail to those later emigrants who used the fort as a jumping-off place. Today the river no longer cuts close to the bank.

State Historical Society of Wisconsin

Below is a photo of "The Rookery" which was built in 1832 and is located on the Main Parade on the hill above the river.

Wilkins crossed the Missouri River here at Old Fort Kearny by taking the ferry across it into the Indian territory of Nebraska. Old Fort Kearny was another of the popular emigrant jumping-off places.

Reproduction of the blockhouse found today in Nebraska City, the location of Old Fort Kearny.

National Park Service

Jackson's painting of the Kanesville Crossing (Council Bluffs) still further upriver with all the wagons lined up waiting for the often unreliable ferries. In 1851 John T. Kerns noted, "On the 10th (May) we tried to get across, but had to give it up as there were too many trains in ahead of us, so we did not get across until the 19th."

This old mill is all that is left of the old Mormon Winter Quarters of 1846-47 which became the site of the Mormon or Upper Ferry, another of the popular crossing areas. The stream that ran the mill is now underground, and the town of Florence, today part of Omaha, was built where the Mormons had lived before their journey to Salt Lake under Brigham Young's leadership in 1847. A beautiful Mormon cemetery is on the bluff above.

Jackson's painting of Alcove Spring just above the Independence Crossing of the Big Blue River on the Independence Road in Kansas. Grandma Sarah Keyes, a member of the Donner party, died here May 29, 1846, and is buried by the road near the old parking lot entrance. Her inscription had originally been carved on a large-spreading oak.

A view of the alcove today. The springs still flow but slowly off on the right side of the photo.

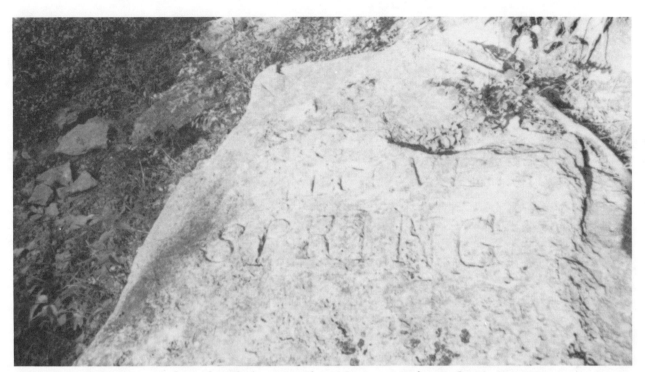

Here you see the rock with the name Alcove Spring carved on it. On May 30, 1846, George McKinstry carved it after Edwin Bryant named it. Both men were also members of the company that included the Donners. Unfortunately, it seems that some modern travelers have tried to improve on the original, and some of the letters have been altered since the photo was taken.

Below is a carving of Reed's name. It could be the one carved by James Reed, another of the Donner party who played an important role in the Donner story. As with Alcove Spring, it seems someone has tried to "improve" on the original.

Hollenberg Ranch house contructed in 1857 right on the trail. It is also one of the few unaltered Pony Express stations.

Twenty miles northwest of the Hollenberg Ranch area the trail came to Rock Creek. This Jackson painting of it seems to be based on a reverse image of the 1859 ambrotype of the East Ranch on the next page.

The earliest photo of Rock Creek Station taken in 1859. The McCanles's built a bridge across the creek where the earlier emigrants had forded. The ranch also served as a stage station and later as a Pony Express station.

The photo below shows the reconstruction of the station that is now underway and is based on the old photo. When finished the park will be an impressive historic park.

Deserted Pawnee village along the Platte was drawn by Wilkins. The village was seen by many emigrants in 1849. Wilkins made the drawing on May 31 as he passed nearby. Bruff passed by on June 12 and also commented about it. It was on the road from old Fort Kearny, seventy-five miles east of new Fort Kearny.

A Jackson photograph of a Pawnee village. This could be the village on the Loup River and was similar to the one abandoned shortly before Wilkins and Bruff visited earlier in 1849.

State Historical Society of Wisconsin

Pawnee Museum in northcentral Kansas. It was built directly over the excavated site of a large Pawnee lodge. Inside many of the artifacts may be seen just as they were left by the Pawnees.

Wilkins drawing of Fort Kearny or Fort Childs, as it was first called. This shows the construction of the fort and is the earliest known drawing, June 4, 1849.

The fort was much larger when Jackson made this romantic version of it in 1866. The fort was about one-half mile from the Platte. As with other military posts or reservations, emigrants were not supposed to camp there. Some diaries refer to an emigrant register kept here during the California gold rush.

Main parade grounds area with the reconstructed blacksmith shop in the background.

Wilkins, it seems, crossed the South Platte on June 13, 1849, in the vicinity of the present I-80 bridge. However, the emigrants crossed the South Platte starting near present-day Hershey, and west along a seventy-five mile stretch wherever the best ford could be found. The two major fording areas were the Lower Ford near Brule, with the trails pulling up the California Hill, or the Upper Crossing near old Julesberg across from Lodgepole Creek.

This is a shot off the I-80 bridge near the area Wilkins would have crossed. Then there were few, if any, trees and the river was deeper and about a mile wide.

Jackson's painting shows the late period crossing of the South Platte near Julesburg, Colorado. This was the major route being used when he went west in 1866. It joined the old trail near Court House Rock. When Jackson crossed the river it was one-half mile wide. Today irrigation has greatly reduced its flow.

This photo shows the swale of the trail near the top of California Hill at the crossing near Brule. The swale is over six feet deep at this section of the trail.

On June 15, Wilkins wrote "Passed to day thro' Ash Hollow, a dry ravine leading to the North Fork, the descent so steep into it that the wagons had to be held back by ropes." Here is the view Wilkins had before he started the steep descent. Notice the scars and deep gullies that were caused by the thousands of wagons that came down the hill. Now erosion has made them even worse.

Below is a view looking back up the hill. On the top of the hill the swales left by the wagons are very evident as they are cut two or three feet into the ridge line.

On June 19 Wilkins stated "Camped tonight in the vicinity of court house rock. This is an immense rock in the shape of buildings standing alone on the prairie, about four miles to the left of the road. Although the distance is so deceptive it does not seem to be more than 1 mile away, and many were the mistakes made by the men in going on foot to see it, most of them turning back after walking a mile or two, apparently getting no nearer. From the point I left the road it must have been six miles. took a sketch of it."

Below is a modern view. Wilkins could have been just off the present highway less than a mile from the entrance to the display near the rocks.

On June 19 Wilkins came within sight of Chimney Rock. On the twentieth he made his sketch. Writing on the twenty-first he said: "Passed Chimney Rock yesterday. it is 12 miles from the court house. took our noon rest within 1 mile of it. it is a singular formation about 200 feet high, but as I took a sketch of it, I shall not trouble you with a description."

State Historical Society of Wisconsin

Below is a photo of the area. Notice how much smaller the chimney looks today. Much has eroded and fallen off since 1849. There are even stories that the army once used it for target practice. Even so, it still was exaggerated some when compared to the nearby bluffs. The photo was taken just off highway 26 near the same area where Jackson made his sketch and famous painting.

Approach to Scotts Bluff taken from Piercy's *Route from Liverpool to Great Salt Lake Valley*. At one time buffalo roamed along the entire Platte Valley from the central plains to the Rockies.

Today there are still buffalo in the area, but only at the zoo in Scotts Bluff. The farms shown here are slowly being pushed back, and housing projects are now devouring the prairie land where the buffalo once grazed.

Famous Mitchell Pass through Scotts Bluff, which was made for the first time replacing the old route through Robidoux Pass. The painting is another of Jackson's.

Today you can walk along the swale of the trail for more than a mile. The photo shows a similar view.

State Historical Society of Wisconsin

Wilkins visited Fort John (Laramie) on June 24, 1849. His drawing shows the fort well maintained.

The photo below shows only a remnant of the adobe Fort John of 1841. It was taken in 1858 when the fort was ten years older and falling apart. The army had purchased this "second Fort Laramie" in 1849 and immediately began new construction.

Library of Congress

69. FORT LARAMIE.

Jackson photo of Fort Laramie taken from approximately the same spot as the earlier one only about twelve years later. Notice the extensive changes in the fort.

The photo below was taken from the same area. Notice the growth of trees along the river and its slightly altered course.

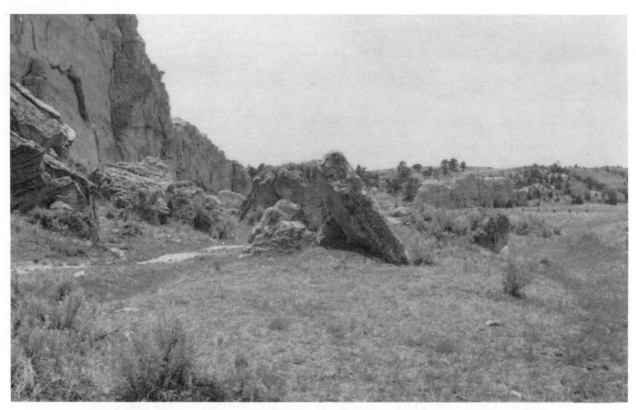

Here is "Register Cliff" where the trail cut close to the bluffs, and the emigrants wrote their names. Note the swale to the right passing the rocks.

Less than a mile further west the trail was forced over the bluffs by the river. Here the wagon wheels cut deeply into the rock, and the route is clear. This is part of the "Oregon Trail Ruts Display" area.

A few days west of Fort Laramie, Wilkins made this drawing at Laramie Peak, the major landmark west of the fort. Many emigrants, however, first reported seeing it for the first time from one of the passes at Scotts Bluff.

Below is a photo from near the same location.

Wilkins called this *Red Hills*. The painting shows the trail as it approached Wagon Hound Creek Crossing, located about nine miles south of Douglas on highway 94. William Baker called the area "Uncle Sam's brick yard" and said that "there is between 3 and 4 miles of road that is as red as a brick and the hills around are the same color."

Today power lines mar the beauty of the area.

Although Wilkins' diary and sketches were usually dated, he often made mistakes with the day and date. Sometimes the labeled date was even off by ten days. This drawing might be one of those cases. The photo below is of Sidley Peak and looks much like his drawing, but his date would put him near Deer Creek, about two days and sixty miles further down the trail. However, the geography of that area doesn't match the drawing.

State Historical Society of Wisconsin

Wilkins probably crossed the North Platte a few miles west of Deer Creek. This area around present-day Glenrock was the first crossing area of the North Platte. It was also one of the most dangerous with many drownings being recorded. The last crossing of the North Platte was west of Casper at Red Buttes or Bessemer Bend.

Along the North Platte at one of the crossing sites at Deer Creek. However, today the river is narrower and trees cover the riverbank at Deer Creek.

Jackson's Fort Caspar and the Platte River Bridge and a photo of the reconstructed fort today. The original trading post and bridge were first constructed here in 1858 and burned by the Indians in 1867.

State Historical Society of Wisconsin

Wilkins made this drawing of the south side of Independence Rock on July 10, 1849. Note again his tendency to add height to his drawings as is evident when compared with the present photo below. Wilkins wrote that "it is a solid dome of granite rising out of the prairie, with thousands of names, painted principally with tar." Today one can still see some of the names cut into the rock that Father DeSmet called "the Great Register of the Desert."

Jackson photo of the rock from the north side and a corresponding photo today. Little seems to have changed in the area.

National Archives #57-HS-285

Early Jackson photo showing the trail passing the north side of Independence Rock looking back east. The trail shows clearly although its use had dropped by 1870 when the photo was made.

The same view of Independence Rock today. A new interpretive display has been built on the west side right next to one of the many parallel swales of the trail, and it deserves a visit by all modern "emigrants."

This Jackson photo was the basis for one of his paintings of Independence Rock. This shows the view looking back east along the trail and Sweetwater. Examining the photo below it seems only the person is different and the river channel has meandered a little.

On July 26, 1849, J. Goldsborough Bruff, like other emigrants, climbed the rock and enjoyed the view. His drawing is looking more to the south when compared to Jackson's.

On June 8, 1850, Charles W. Smith, a former newspaperman on his way to California, wrote, "I climbed up its abrupt rocky sides, and spent a few minutes walking about its summit, though I had not time to examine it as I wished." You also can climb the rock to examine it. Take your time. The view is beautiful, but watch your hat, the wind really blows up there.

The pass through the Rattlesnake Mountains, as J. Goldsborough Bruff saw it on July 26, 1849. Below an older highway follows the old trail, but today the new road bypasses it. There is a new interpretive display where one can look back at Sweetwater Pass and also Devil's Gate.

Bruff's Devils Gate. It was a curiosity for the emigrants. Smith said that "some of our party climbed to the top of the Gate and boasted of having done some daring climbing." Sometimes a few unfortunates fell. Others walked or tried to walk through. Almost all commented on its size.

Wilkin's mentioned that "the sides of the gap are so perpendicular. . .they are very high and rugid." He regretted that he "could not pass two or three hours here to finish the sketch of it more highly." His painting based on the sketch is below.

Jackson's photo was from nearly the same place that Bruff used in his sketch.

Today it seems little has changed at Devil's Gate. The feeling of excitement and curiosity experienced by the emigrants can still be felt today. The first drawing of it was made by Alfred J. Miller in 1837.

Wilkins made this panoramic view of the Sweetwater Valley a few miles further up the river. Here is the *Old Man* or *Great Stone Face* as known today, but called *Sweet Water Buttes* by Wilkins. Split Rock is now at the extreme right in the painting.

When Wilkins traveled through here he wrote "Grass very scarce the camping places, as laid down in the guide books as having plenty of grass. we have invariably found none there. it being all eaten off by previous trains." As a result of the conditions, he noted many dead animals and ejected property along the trail in this section. Today the relics are gone, there is more grass, but the ranchers still lose animals along there.

National Archives #57-HS-299

Two Jackson photos taken near Three Crossings. Above shows the abandoned Three Crossings Stage Station and below another shot a little further west showing the grave of a soldier, Bennett Tribbetts, killed in 1862. The photo above was the basis for his painting of *Three Crossings*.

National Archives #57-HS-246

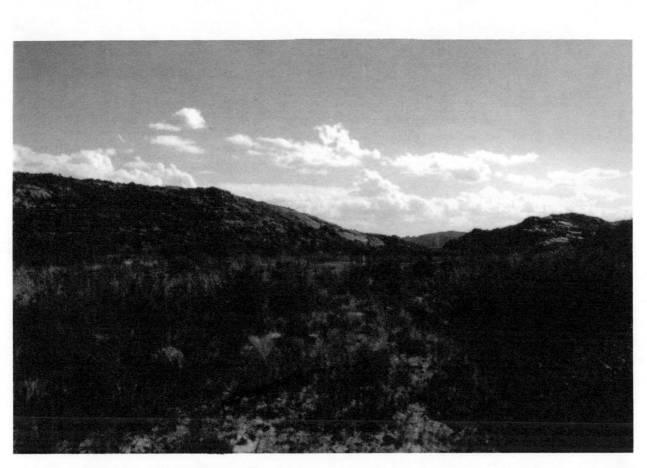

Here are corresponding photos to the ones made by Jackson in 1870. You can almost feel Jackson's presence.

Wilkins took the Three Crossing's route and made this drawing of it near where the trail was forced to make its second of the three crossings. Today the willows have overgrown the riverbanks. The early emigrants would not have found these. Any wood would have been cut.

The emigrant's first view of the Rockies. Wilkins drew this on July 12, 1849. It is about nine miles west of Three Crossings as the trail comes back down to the Sweetwater for its fifth fording or crossing.

Note once again the artist's "liberties" taken by exaggerating the height of the Wind River Mountains when compared to the photo below in which they aren't even visible because of pollution today.

State Historical Society of Wisconsin

This section of the trail was often written about but rarely drawn. This is the Rocky Ridge that caused many a problem for the emigrants. Wilkins painted this view.

Even today a modern four-by-four has trouble negotiating the rocks. The early emigrants walked this unless they were very sick riding in the wagons. Even today it is smoother walking.

Jackson's painting of the trail about a mile after it crossed the Sweetwater for the last time. On the left horizon are the famous Twin Mounds and off to the right would be the Wind River Mountains. About eight miles ahead lies the great South Pass. Little has changed in this area since the emigrants passed.

The famous Pacific Springs—the first water west of the South Pass, only about three miles from the summit. Few emigrants stopped at the pass—many could not tell it was the pass—but most wanted to get to the water that ran to the Pacific.

Below is the scene today. Pacific Creek shows up clearly. The springs and the ruins from the Old Halter and Flick Ranch are to the right just off the photo and painting.

This is a pen sketch containing the following handwritten annotations:

Upper sketch:
- Looking back toward S. Pass.
- Wind R. Mounts about 15 mi.
- snow
- bl sh gr & snow patches
- d slate
- r sh
- r sh gr
- q r & p g
- r sh br cliffs

Lower sketch:
- b sh olive
- y sh gr on top
- b & r sh g
- wagons
- dust
- d gr
- wagons
- faded swamp &
- sage
- sage

This pen sketch of Bruff's shows the South Pass area looking back east toward Pacific Springs and the pass.

The photo shows the same area with the Wind River Mountains on the left.

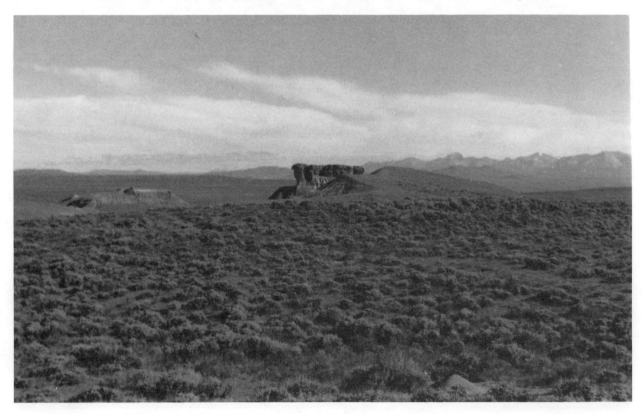

Clay: Banks opp. the gravel Bluff where
I obtain'd felspar fragments
A
On right — d cr sh   A. M.
fwdh   cr sh

Bruff made this pencil sketch of "Plume Rock" named because of its shape and colors. It is located where the trail turned northwest toward the Dry Sandy Crossing. Today the balanced "rock" has been eroded and fallen off, and a hawk nests on the plume.

Jackson's painting of South Pass, "Approach to the Dry Sandy" was probably made about a mile past Plume Rock, as the trail approached the crossing of the Dry Sandy. A few miles west of here the Sublette Cutoff branches off while the old trail continues down to Fort Bridger.

State Historical Society of Wisconsin

Wilkins made this drawing of the trail as it came into the Green River Valley, on his way to Fort Bridger. Here is a photo of one of the sites where the trail drops down to the flat river bottom as it approaches the Lombard Ferry area.

Wilkins appears to have crossed the Green River down at the Lombard Ferry. Each year the specific location of the ferry may have changed a little with changing river conditions. Today the location is part of a bird sanctuary, and a new highway bridge has been built in the area.

Cathedral Rock or Church Butte was a noted landmark on the trail to Fort Bridger after crossing the Ham's Fork River. Here is Wilkins' painting labelled Cathedral Rock as he saw it on July 24. The photo shows the "rock" today. It seems to have eroded some, or he "squared" it off to look better.

Jackson made this photo of Cathedral Rock or Church Butte from a different angle, looking back east at it.

Here is Cathedral Rock from the same position, and now it shows little erosion, even the sage looks the same.

Jackson made this sketch looking west toward Fort Bridger and Bridger Butte on July 4, 1867. He was on his return trip from California and a few miles east of the fort.

Below is a photo taken from near the same location.

When Jackson first visited Fort Bridger it was a military post. He never saw the original trading post of Jim Bridger. However, here is his version of the early Fort Bridger.

This drawing of Fort Bridger is taken from Stansbury's, *An Expedition to the Valley of the Great Salt Lake of Utah* (1852). Note the similarities with the later Jackson painting.

Wilkins's painting of Fort Bridger. He described it as "is merely a few log houses built in a square . . . a few goods are kept for sale here at most exorbitant prices."

Below is a view more like those by Stansbury and Jackson. Note Bridger Butte in the background.

The beginning section of the Hastings Cutoff from Fort Bridger headed southwest down Echo Canyon. It later became part of the Mormon Road or Salt Lake Trail. Jackson took this route on his trip to California. He returned a few years later and took this photo. Note the railroad constructed parallel to the trail almost on top of it.

The photo below shows the "Amphitheatre" area today.

National Archives #57-HS-31

Another Jackson photo from further down the canyon looking back up the trail at the "Great Eastern." He also made a painting of the same spot.

Below is a photo of the area today. The "old" modern highway and railroad that cuts through today has widened the base of the canyon. For the emigrants there were some places that were only wide enough for a wagon. Today the interstate also follows the same general route.

Jackson's drawing showing the trail as it approached the junction of Echo and Weber canyons.

The same view today. Now the interstate, railroad, and earlier highway all run parallel and on top of the old trail.

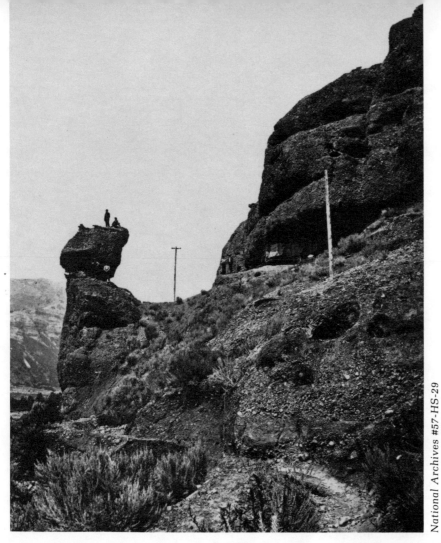

National Archives #57-HS-29

Pulpit Rock marked the mouth of Echo Canyon. Brigham Young spoke from here on his journey to Salt Lake. Jackson made this early photograph of others who climbed the rock.

Note the changes in the area today. Pulpit Rock was destroyed to make room for the modern highway and railroad.

Jackson photograph showing Devil's Slide in the Weber Canyon. The early trail passed this, but after the Donner party cut a new route over the mountains the Weber route was used less and less.

Devil's Slide today.

National Park Service

Jackson's painting of the entrance into the Great Salt Lake Valley.

Below is a photo of Emigration Canyon as the trail came down the mountains. This canyon passage was very difficult. It was also part of the trail blazed by the Donners.

Jackson's painting of Parley Canyon. This became the major route and bypassed the parallel section down Emigration Canyon.

Today the modern interstate follows part of the same route down Parley Canyon to Salt Lake City.

Returning to the Green River, this is another of the ferries that developed along the Green River. It appears to be the Case Ferry on the Baker-Davis Cutoff. It is taken from Ghent's *The Road to Oregon*. This cutoff was one of the variants developed to bypass both the long dip in the trail to Fort Bridger and also the dry Sublette crossing. It joins the Slate Creek and Sublette Cutoff.

The photo below shows the area today. An unnamed grave is located near where the photo was taken.

Butte in distance, approaching it

A fossiliferous clay Mount, bearing W.S.W. on the desert march of Sublette's Cut-off, (Greenwood's Cut-off (called improperly by the Emigrants Sublette) between Big Sandy & Green River; Wind-River chain on right, and distant Bear River Mts. ahead. The Butte is near 100ft. high.

On August 4, 1849 Bruff made this drawing of Haystack Butte. This was a landmark on the Sublette Cutoff which separated from the trail to Fort Bridger a few miles west of the Dry Sandy Crossing.

It seems to look pretty much the same today only eroded a little more. His painting, unfortunately, made it appear slightly larger than his original more accurate pen drawing.

*Terminus of the Greenwood
Cut off. — descent into Green
River valley —*

Bruff made this sketch on the "Descent to the Green" after crossing Sublettes Flat. The drop off was sharp and the emigrants descended in a variety of places where they felt safe.

Below is a picture of one of those places. It may not look very steep but from sitting in the driver's seat one could not see the trail over the hood for half the descent. You had to "feel" your way down. There is no doubt, it is *steep*.

138

Bruff drew this Indian diagram he discovered carved on the bluffs in the area.
These are not the same ones but come from the same area.

The handwritten annotations on the sketch read:

Bluffs on La Fontenelle — Camp. Aug 7th 1849

Cliff of Sand Stone, Cont.g galena.
About 500' high
(w clouds)

dr blue

Buff, orangey bluish, & white, in horizontal strata, orange at top Vertical face, overhanging in places.

Sand & scattering sage bushes.

Sage

Road

Once across the Green River the trail cut southwest along the river and then over the bluffs to Fontenelle's Creek. Above is Bruff's sketch of "Fontenelle Bluffs" near the Green.

Below is a photo of the area today. It looks the same today as when Bruff was there.

Here we are back on the main part of the trail heading north toward Fort Hall. Wilkin's made this drawing of the trail after it climbed the "Big Hill" and descended into the valley of the Bear River again just east of the present town of Dingle Station.

Below is a photo of the area today. Note the scars on the mountain and the farm road at the base.

Wilkins continued up the Bear River Valley. He recorded this scene as the "Bear River Peaks."

Below is a photo taken off the main intersection in Cokeville. The trail pretty much coincides with U.S. Highway 30 from south of Montpelier north all the way to Soda Point.

A few days later on August 2 Wilkins camped at present-day Bennington and saw the sunrise and recorded it as "Bear Mountain Sunrise." Baldy is the present name given to the larger mountain to the left of center.

Below is present-day Hooper Spring, one of the few left in the area today. When drinking from some of the springs Wilkins noted that "we took our tin cups and some sugar and drank repeated draughts of excellent soda water." He also said the water was "impregnated with oxide of Iron." The modern emigrant can drink from the spring as those earlier ones had done. Use some Tang and you won't notice the taste of iron.

State Historical Society of Wisconsin

Wilkins's painting of the Soda Springs area. Palmer in 1845 and Ingersoll in 1847 noted many large white mounds some with soda water in them between fifteen and thirty feet tall off to the right of the trail. In 1849 Bryarly wrote extensively about them. Today the town of Soda Springs has developed, the cones have been graded away, and the Bear River has been dammed. Even the famous Steamboat Spring and geyser have been flooded by the river.

Below is a cone in another city park similar to those seen and climbed by the early emigrants.

Bruff's drawing of Fort Hall. When the scene was larger than his paper allowed, he drew the rest under it and put an "X" where the two segments joined.

146

Jackson's painting of Fort Hall and a photo of the Fort Hall replica that is located in Ross Park south of Pocatello. Jackson never saw the original Fort Hall. His painting is similar to Bruff's sketch and also to one by William Henry Tappan.

Bruff made this sketch of the trail along the Snake River as it approached the area now called Massacre Rocks. The usage of the present name first appeared in the early 1900s but was based on some Indian attacks on emigrant trains in the area in 1862. The passage was only wide enough for one wagon when Bruff went through. The modern interstate highway has widened the opening considerable. In 1849 Bryarly described the area: "The banks of the river here is well marked, being high rocky bluffs, resembling those of the beautiful Hudson River. Six miles from Falls, the road passes through two 'Buttes' of solid rock with just space between for the road."

The view still looks pretty much the same except for the modern highway. There is also a park in the area today.

Wilkins, it seems, made many sketches of "City of the Rocks" but none have survived. He was one of the first to use that name for the area. Many emigrants commented on the rocks, and the area was known by many names—Pyramid Valley, Valley of the Rocks, etc. Some emigrants even painted names on the rock; one of the larger ones was called "City Hotel" and another "Castle Rock." The photos are from today.

Singular formations of

No sign yet of any / left our in / train. A [left margin]

Sareoph. / Cave / rock

Night very cold, hardly / slept. — On guard — with — / took laudanum [right margin]

disintegrate / granite or sienite / another / sketch will show

a party of Illinoiseans — 7 persons mounted, and 1 mule wagon from Salt Lake — heard of friends McNulty & Co — "Spire Rock" — 1 side of outlet, gate of a valley; ½ mile beyond Salt L^e road comes in. Travell'd till after sunset — 3 dead Oxen. Camp'd near an old Sps. and groves of willows, &c. Sun set clr. Wind mod. W. 58°.

Bruff made this sketch of some formations in this valley. He described them as "singular formations of disintegrated granite" and on August 29, 1849 rested in a cavelike portion of one he called "Sarcophagus Rock."

The rotated text on the right reads "Yale University, Beinecke Rare Book and Manuscript Library"

Here are the same rocks today. Bruff would feel right at home.

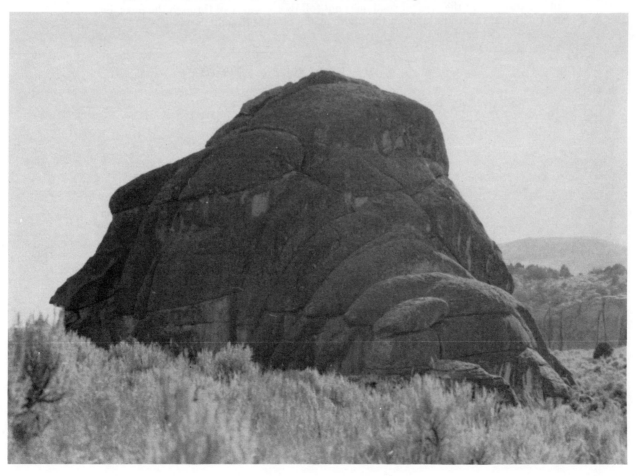

Bluff's sketch of the trail heading for Pinnacle Pass as it leaves City of Rocks. The photo shows that the present road does not follow the old trail through the pass, but leaves it just off to the right of the photo at the base of Steeple Rock.

Photos of the area today. The faint scar of the trail is visible in the photo above. If you were to walk through the pass you could see where wagons left their marks on the rocks.

California Historical Society

This famous landmark called "Steeple Rock" by the emigrants or "Twin Sisters" today. This marked the junction of the Salt Lake Road, first blazed by Sam Hensley, and the California Trail coming down from Fort Hall and the Hudspeth's Cutoff. The sketch was made in the 1850s from an early daugerrotype.

The present photo was taken near the junction of the trails. The immediate area has changed very little.

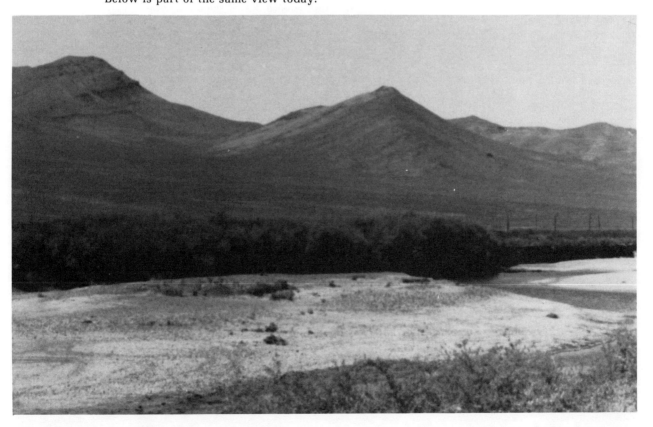

Bruff's sketch of Battle Mountain or Shoshone Mesa along the Humboldt or Mary's River.
Below is part of the same view today.

Rabbit Hole Spring an important watering place on the Applegate-Lassen Route. Like many other springs along the trail dead and dying animals littered the area. The rotting carcasses often spoiled the water. Bruff shows this in his sketch and also commented about the bloated carcasses and those stuck in the watering holes.

Below is the same area today. A spring house covers one of the old springs.

A similar scene from a different watering hole further east on the trail today. Death was always nearby.

Bruff made this sketch of the Black Rock Desert on the Lassen Road. It was dry and hot, and the only water after crossing the desert were some hot springs at the base of the Black Rock.

Below is the area today. It is still dangerous and desolate to travel even today. Don't travel there alone.

O. Dist.

warm y.

l blue

d. bl. &c.

y. sh w stripe

Straw col.

About N. W. by W. from Black Rock: —

Fremonts' Castle w/ singular formation

ention'd 4 pages back) (about opposite to mirage)

y. sh. brush g.

r

debris

Sage bushes

A little further up the trail Bruff wrote on September 23, 1849 "across the valley to the N. by W. was a very remarkable resemblance of a castle or fortress, of a white substance, (probably clay), in the face of a brownish hill, resting on a shelf of rock, about 1/3 from the plain; This I sketch'd, and named it Fremont's Castle."

Here it is today. Bruff's drawing seems more impressive than the real thing.

Descent into pass. 25th —

Impassable Cañon, save to foot animals

CAÑON

※ *The spiry rock - highest of this extraordinary wall, in the base of which is this cavern, gives name to the Cañon - "High Rock".*

The well-known "Descent to Fly Canyon" sketched by Bruff on September 25. He noted the steep descent and the broken wagons littering the bottom.

Below is a photo of the area today. Even walking down the hill was difficult. One of Bruff's later paintings, however, made it appear larger and steeper than it is. Again it seems his sketches were more accurate than his paintings.

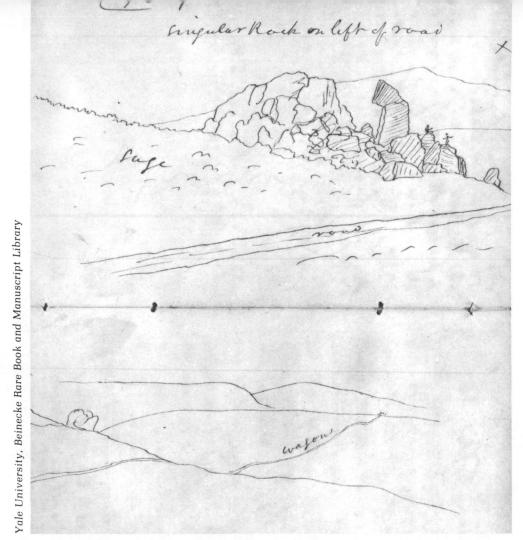

singular Rock on left of road

sage

road

wagon

This formation of rocks was called "Singular Rock" by Bruff. Below is the same scene today. Little has changed in the area. Only one of the rocks has fallen over, and the trail is overgrown.

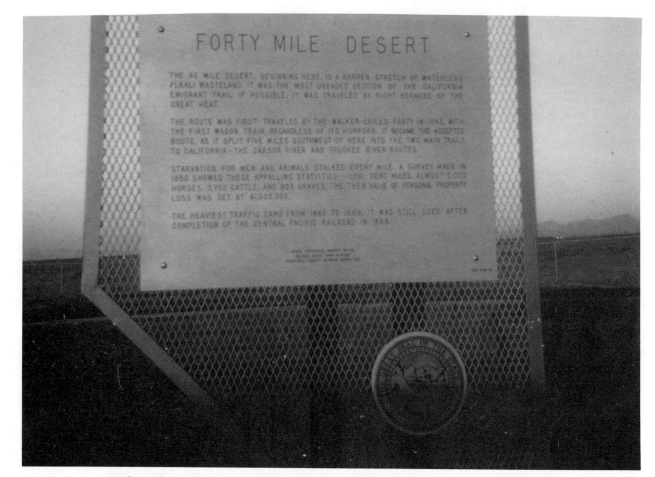

FORTY MILE DESERT

THE 40 MILE DESERT, BEGINNING HERE, IS A BARREN STRETCH OF WATERLESS
ALKALI WASTELAND. IT WAS THE MOST DREADED SECTION OF THE CALIFORNIA
EMIGRANT TRAIL. IF POSSIBLE, IT WAS TRAVELED BY NIGHT BECAUSE OF THE
GREAT HEAT.

THE ROUTE WAS FIRST TRAVELED BY THE WALKER-CHILES PARTY IN 1843. WITH
THE FIRST WAGON TRAIN, REGARDLESS OF ITS HORRORS, IT BECAME THE ACCEPTED
ROUTE, AS IT SPLIT FIVE MILES SOUTHWEST OF HERE INTO THE TWO MAIN TRAILS
TO CALIFORNIA — THE CARSON RIVER AND TRUCKEE RIVER ROUTES.

STARVATION FOR MEN AND ANIMALS STALKED EVERY MILE. A SURVEY MADE IN
1850 SHOWED THESE APPALLING STATISTICS—1061 DEAD MULES, ALMOST 5,000
HORSES, 3,750 CATTLE, AND 953 GRAVES. THE THEN VALUE OF PERSONAL PROPERTY
LOSS WAS SET AT $1,000,000.

THE HEAVIEST TRAFFIC CAME FROM 1849 TO 1869. IT WAS STILL USED AFTER
COMPLETION OF THE CENTRAL PACIFIC RAILROAD IN 1869.

Back on the main trail down the Humboldt. The Applegate-Lassen Route turned off earlier at the meadows. This is the Forty-Mile Desert which started after the Humboldt sink and it proved to be as bad as, if not worse, than the Black Rock Desert. (See Diary Section.)

After crossing the desert one branch of the trail followed the Truckee up the Sierra Nevada. Here is the monument at Donner Pass State Park where the Donner party spent their fateful winter.

This large rock was the wall for one of the cabins built. Today it has a marker with the names of the Donner party members.

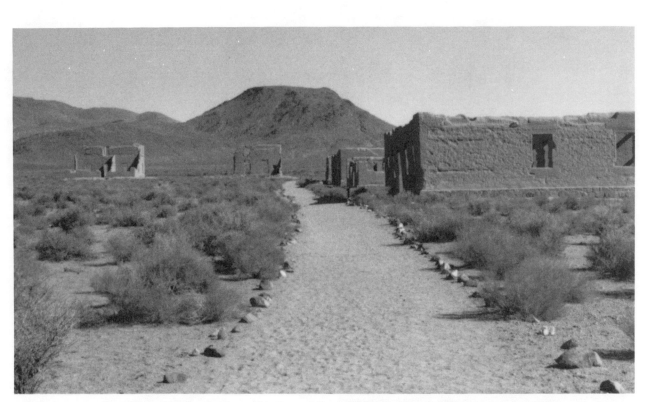

Fort Churchill was built on the Carson Route in 1860. Here are the remnants of the fort.

Below is a reconstruction of the Mormon Station that was built around 1850. Both these places helped many an emigrant after the desert crossing and before the long pull over the Sierra Nevada crossing.

A drawing of the trail through the Carson Canyon going up the mountain. Then it was a very difficult passage. Today the modern road has cut out the twists and turns and most of the river crossings.

Sutter's Fort. The center of the new empire called "New Helvetia," and the goal of most of the early emigrants. Here they found a helpful hand after their long hard journey across the plains, deserts, and mountains.

Sutter's Fort as it appears today. Once in the middle of nowhere, it is now built up all around and in the city of Sacramento. Only when you are inside can you get a sense of what it was like many years ago.

James Marshall, who discovered gold on January 24, 1848 at Sutter's Mill four years later. By then California had changed more than either Marshall or Sutter would have thought back in 1848.

Today the mill has been reconstructed near its original location in Coloma the town that grew up around the site. The stream has changed its course since the gold rush.

California Historical Society

An early drawing of Placerville or Hangtown. This was the end of the trail for many of the gold seekers and Betsey and Ike.

Below is a photo of Placerville today.

Alfred J. Miller's painting of Joseph R. Walker. He was possibly the most famous and successful of the mountain men. Walker helped Bonneville in the 1830s and Fremont in the 1840s. He was the first to really explore the Great Basin, even more than Smith did. He opened up much of what became the California Trail, discovered the Walker Pass, and was the first white man in Yosemite Valley. He helped guide many an emigrant to California.

Jim Beckwourth was the son of a slave and southern planter. He became a mountain man and later guide for the emigrants. He discovered the Beckwourth Pass across the Sierra Nevada.

Elisha Stephens was another mountain man and guide. He led the first successful wagon train over the Sierra Nevada into California in 1844. This is the only known photograph of Stephens taken in 1864.

John Sutter. His dream was to create his own empire. He was well on his way until the discovery of gold and the takeover of California by the United States. Both of these events caused Sutter more problems than benefits. Sutter's fate was like that of John McLoughlin's of Oregon—both men helped the early emigrants and both lost their empires and neither completely recovered.

LANSFORD WARREN HASTINGS

Author of "Emigrant's Guide to Oregon and California."
Personally guided the first emigrant train across the
Great Salt Desert in 1846.

REPRODUCED FROM THE ONLY KNOWN PHOTOGRAPH, THROUGH COURTESY
OF MR. ALBERT SPENCE, LOS ANGELES

Lansford Hastings also dreamed of creating an empire for himself. However, he is most remembered for his guidebook, the infamous Hastings Cutoff, and its association with the Donner disaster.

James Marshall, the man who actually discovered the gold that fateful day January 24, 1848 at Sutter's Mill. California was never the same again.

Winter in S. Nevada
Auth. Author on Snow-Shoes, seeking fuel

J. Goldsborough Bruff, the man who led a wagon company west in 1849 and made many of the drawings and paintings included in this book.

James and Margaret Reed. They are the emigrants associated with the Donner party of 1846. James led one of the relief parties that helped bring back his wife and family.

Museums and Displays

There are a number of museums and points of interest along the highways that parallel or intersect the old California Trail that the modern traveler can visit to learn more about the westward journey and the experiences of the emigrants. Thirty-two of the more important places are here identified. They range from major population centers with many different historic sites to individual interpretive sites along the highway. Some may be visited in a half hour while at others one can easily spend a whole day.

Jefferson National Expansion Memorial, St. Louis, Missouri

Independence, Missouri and Kansas City Vicinity

Fort Leavenworth, Kansas

Weston, Missouri—Historic District

St. Joseph, Missouri Vicinity

Council Bluffs and Omaha Vicinity

Hollenberg Ranch, Kansas

Pawnee Indian Village, Kansas

Rock Creek Station, Nebraska

Fort Kearny, Nebraska

Ash Hollow, Nebraska

Court House and Chimney Rock, Nebraska Rock, Nebraska

Scotts Bluff National Monument, Nebraska

Fort Laramie, Wyoming

* Register Cliff & Oregon Trail Ruts, Wyoming

Fort Caspar, Wyoming

* Independence Rock, Wyoming
* Devil's Gate, Wyoming
* Split Rock, Wyoming
* South Pass, Wyoming

Fort Bridger, Wyoming

Pioneer Trail State Park, Utah

* Soda Springs, Idaho

Fort Hall, Idaho

Northeastern Nevada Museum, Nevada

Fort Churchill State Historic Monument, Nevada

Mormon Station Historic State Monument, Nevada

Donner Memorial State Park, California

* Lassen Volcanic National Park, California

Sutter's Fort, California

Marshall Gold Discovery State Historic Park, California

Placerville, California—Historic District

* Interpretive displays only

Jefferson National Expansion Memorial, St. Louis Missouri

Here is the location of the gigantic Gateway Arch, which commemorates St. Louis as the "Gateway to the West." It is located on the site of old St. Louis. Under the arch is the location of the Museum of Westward Expansion. In it can be found exhibits that cover the whole period of westward expansion and development including the California Trail era. It begins with displays of the Lewis and Clark Expedition's exploration of the West and continues with the Indians, the trappers, the emigrants, the cowboys, the homesteaders, and the railroads until the West was settled and "closed."

The park is located on the west bank of the Mississippi River just off I-55 and I-70, and other points of historical interest are also within walking distance of the memorial park.

Independence, Missouri and Kansas City Vicinity

This area is the location of the beginning of the trails west, whether it was to the Santa Fe, Oregon, and California routes. There are many different museums, historic buildings, and points of interest within the area, which can take a few days to visit and enjoy. Independence Square is often considered to be the starting point for the trails. Here is the present-day courthouse, which contains parts of the early courthouse as shown in the pictorial section of this book. Spring Park is near the square and contains one of the earliest structures built in Independence, the Brady cabin. Other homes from the 1850s are now open, such as the Wornall and Harris houses. Cave Spring in Klein Park, Jim Bridger's grave, and Old Westport are all found here. The Shawnee Methodist Mission has been reopened and was a place often visited by early emigrants before they began their trek onto the vast prairies. The Kansas State Historical Society has just finished several years of extensive restoration of this mission. All of these historical landmarks, many well-known to the emigrants, relate to the period of the opening of the trails west.

Fort Leavenworth, Kansas

This is the oldest continuously operated military post west of the Mississippi. It was first constructed in 1827. This area became one of the jumping-off places for the emigrants. On his way to California in 1849 James Wilkins, the artist, drew a picture of this post. Today the post museum, with its emphasis on its military role and the opening of the West to traders and emigrants can be visited; one can also walk on the main parade ground that was the site of early councils with the Indians. At this time the fort is also the location of the Command and General Staff College for advanced military training.

It is located off highway 73 just north of present-day Leavenworth, Kansas, which was first named Douglas City in 1854.

Weston, Missouri

During the early years of the gold rush Weston was one of the major embarking areas for the emigrants. It was even considered to be one of the greatest port cities of the future. However, due to flooding and a change in the river channel, Weston was left "high and dry" and today is about two miles from the river. The town is presently a Registered Historic District and has a nice museum. In addition there are numerous buildings from its heyday period, and many of the older homes are periodically open to the public. You can stand at the main intersection and also imagine the riverboats pulling up to the area where the railroad tracks now run.

The town is located in Missouri off state highway 45, a few miles northeast of Leavenworth, Kansas.

St. Joseph, Missouri, Vicinity

The St. Joseph Museum has displays that depict the role of the town in the period of westward expansion, the Indians, and the Civil War. Also within St. Joseph is the Pony Express Stables Museum, which is devoted to the history of the town with an emphasis on the Pony Express period.

They are respectively located at Eleventh and Charles Street, and 914 Penn Street.

Council Bluffs and Omaha Vicinity

This area was another of the jumping-off places for the emigrants, and the principal point of departure for emigrants following the north side of the Platte River. It was also the "Winter Quarters" for the Mormons in 1846-47. The old Mormon Cemetery is located on Thirty-sixth and State Street as is a small visitor center for those interested in the Mormon history of the trail. Nearby is the site of the Mormon Ferry and the old mill, which should be restored. The Josely Art Museum is also in Omaha and includes excellent exhibits on early Indian life and early expeditions in that area. It is located at 2200 Dodge Street.

Hollenberg Ranch, Hanover, Kansas

A Kansas State historic site, this ranch was constructed by Gerat Hollenberg, a German emigrant, who had originally gone west to the gold diggings of California but left there after not having much success. He came to Kansas in 1847 and made this location his ranch. It was situated on the main California-Oregon Trail west of the junctions of the Independence, St. Joseph, and Fort Leavenworth roads. The structure is unaltered and has a small museum in it. It served as a store for emigrants, a stage station, and later as a Pony Express station. The museum is primarily devoted to its role in the Pony Express venture.

Its location is about one mile east of Hanover on Kansas 243.

Pawnee Indian Village, Kansas

A Kansas State historic site. While this museum is off the California Trail, it is included because many of the emigrants to California remarked about seeing an old abandoned Pawnee village along the Platte River. James Wilkins's drawing of it is included in the pictorial section of this volume as is a Jackson photograph of a Pawnee village. It is possible that this photo shows the new village, which was established after the older one was abandoned. The museum was constructed over the site of one of the larger lodges of the village, and the floor of the lodge can be viewed with the artifacts left as they were uncovered by the archeologists. This museum is devoted to showing how the Pawnee Indians lived in this region of northern Kansas and southern Nebraska during the 1800s when the emigrants were traveling through the area.

The museum is run by the Kansas State Historical Society and is located about three miles southwest of Republic, Kansas, about fifty miles west of Hanover.

Rock Creek Station, Nebraska

A Nebraska State historic site, Rock Creek Station was first developed in 1857 by S.C. Glenn who built a small cabin and established a store for the emigrants at the ford of Rock Creek. By 1859 David McCanles purchased the place and established a ranch here, later used as a stage and Pony Express station. At the same time he built a bridge across Rock Creek. The ranch is perhaps most famous for its role in the Hickok-McCanles shooting of 1861. Today the area is being developed by the Nebraska Game and Parks Commission, and both the east and west ranches are being reconstructed as they were through to appear in 1859. There is a fine museum, campgrounds, and picnic area. One can also take a short ride in an ox-drawn wagon as the emigrants did. The swale from the thousands of wagons that crossed there are most vivid on the west or north side of the creek.

The park is located about seven miles east of Fairbury off Nebraska Highway 8.

Fort Kearny, Nebraska

Nebraska State historic park. This fort originally called Fort Childs was constructed in 1848 by Lieutenant Woodbury. Today there is a nice museum that shows the history of the post. The blacksmith shop has been reconstructed along with a stockade. One can walk about the grounds and the main parade and see the locations of some of the other buildings. Some of the large trees standing in the parade area were planted by Lieutenant Woodbury in 1848. Also on the grounds is a reconstructed powder magazine that has collapsed. The area around the fort has changed considerably from the emigrants era. Then it was dry and sandy, today with irrigation it is a rich farming area.

It is located south and east of Kearny just west of Nebraska Highway 10.

Ash Hollow, Nebraska

Today this is a State Historical Park. This is where the trail dropped back down to the North Platte River valley after crossing the South Platte and the plateau between the two forks of the Platte. At Windlass Hill one can look at the vivid scars of the trail as it comes down the hill. Also in the park is Ash Hollow Spring and a campground is in the park; they're located where emigrants would have camped. The whole period of history of Ash Hollow is covered in a fine interpretive center. Ash Hollow Cemetery has a number of graves from the trail period. (California Hill, where the emigrants first climbed the plateau after crossing the South Platte, can be viewed four miles west of Brule, Nebraska, on U.S. Highway 30. However, there is no display but only a marker, and the most dramatic ruts are on private ground off a farm road.)

Ash Hollow is located on U.S. Highway 26 as it approaches the North Platte from the south.

Court House and Chimney Rock, Nebraska

Both Nebraska State historic sites, these prominent landmarks on the trail are still a wonder to be seen by the modern traveler. In addition, Chimney Rock holds the dual distinction of also being a National Historic

Landmark. Today small mobile displays are located near each. It is the view of them, however, that makes one feel like an emigrant of long ago. Each display has information on the landmarks, and there are staff members who are happy to talk to you.

Both landmarks are in the vicinity of Bridgeport, Nebraska, off highway 92. Court House Rock is about five miles south of Chimney Rock about fifteen miles west.

Scotts Bluff National Monument, Nebraska

The early emigrants did not pass through Mitchell Pass here at Scotts Bluff but traveled a few miles south through Robidoux Pass. There are some markers there noting the location of certain historical sites. This was the route used by the early emigrants and forty-niners on their way to California. Information about Robidoux Pass is included in the Oregon Trail Museum, which is located at the Mitchell Pass Visitor Center. There are living displays there, so you can talk to park attendants playing the roles of emigrants and soldiers. Today, modern emigrants can walk along in the swale of the trail that was opened in 1851 and used heavily after that time. This was also the route later used by the Pony Express and the telegraph. Within the museum itself is one of the finest collections of paintings of scenes along the trail by William Henry Jackson.

The museum and pass is located on highway 92 just west of Gering.

Fort Laramie, Wyoming

Today Fort Laramie is a National Historic Site and has perhaps the best developed displays and museum along the California-Oregon Trail. On the grounds are the Sutler's store and Old Bedlam, both constructed in 1849. Other buildings have also been restored and are full of interesting displays. Plan on spending a few hours there to take in all the displays and to talk to the sutler, the wives of officers and enlisted men, trappers, cavalrymen and others who are part of the living displays.

The fort is located three miles west of the town of Fort Laramie off U.S. Highway 26.

Register Cliff and Oregon Trail Ruts, Wyoming

Wyoming State historic sites. These two spots have no museums but include the physical evidence of the westward trek. Register Cliff is full of names carved by the emigrants and next to it is a small cemetery. Oregon Trail Ruts is just what it says it is. There are excellent examples of the effect of the thousands of wagons that cut their way west over the hills and rocks. In some places the wagons cut more than three feet into the hills, and the tire and wheel marks are still evident.

Both of these are located near Guernsey off U.S. Highway 26.

Fort Caspar, Wyoming

Within the city of Casper are some important sites. One is Fort Caspar, which has been reconstructed and has many displays. Near it is the new museum that also houses many displays relating to the emigrant period. Also at the fort is a partial reconstruction of the Guinard Bridge, and one can see some of the remains of the earth and log crib on which the rest of the bridge stood. Also within the town are the sites of the Mormon Ferry established in 1847 and the Reshaw Bridge. At present, however, little has been done concerning these sites. Southwest of Casper is another site where the emigrants crossed the North Platte—Bessemer Bend. Today there is a small interpretive display where the emigrants forded the North Platte.

Fort Caspar is located on Fort Caspar Road just before it crosses the North Platte River in the western part of Casper.

Between Fort Caspar and Fort Bridger there are no museums, but there are a number of interpretive sites at major landmarks along the trail and these will be identified. Such landmarks helped to keep the emigrants and trappers heading in the right direction. Interestingly, the city of Casper was named in honor of Lt. Caspar Collins, but was misspelled in the process.

Independence Rock, Wyoming

Wyoming State historic site. Independence Rock rivals Chimney Rock,

Nebraska as claimant to being the most famous of all trail landmarks. Many of the names of emigrants and trappers that are over a century old can still be found on this rock. One can climb the rock as many emigrants surely did. The site is located about fifty miles west of Casper on Wyoming Highway 220.

Devil's Gate, Wyoming

This was a famous landmark and curiosity to the westward emigrant. Many took time to try to either climb to the top of walk through it. Today it is on private grounds, but you can view the area from a new interpretive site about five miles west of Independence Rock on Wyoming Highway 220.

Split Rock, Wyoming

This was another landmark along the trail. It later became the site of a Pony Express station. The display is located on U.S. Highway 287.

South Pass, Wyoming

Unfortunately this interpretive site has been the subject of much vandalism. It is about four miles west of the actual pass on highway 28, about 45 miles southwest of Lander. One can look back east of it to Pacific Springs and South Pass.

Fort Bridger, Wyoming

This was the location of Bridger's and Vasquez's early trading posts. Today it is a State Historic Site, but nothing is left of Bridger's earlier posts. The buildings that survive and have been restored are from its military period. The museum is fine, and the restoration of many of the remaining buildings is continuing.

It was here at Fort Bridger that the emigrants had to decide whether to go by way of Salt Lake or Fort Hall.

Fort Bridger is located off I-80 in the western part of the town of Fort Bridger.

Pioneer Trail State Park, Utah

This park is on the branch of the trail into Salt Lake City in Emigration Canyon. There is a visitor center and picnic grounds available for the modern traveler. Most of the displays are related to the Mormon

migration along this route and the pioneer development of the area. "Old Desert," a recreated pioneer village, shows life from 1847-69, and it also includes Brigham Young's farmhouse. Here is the Mormon monument, This Is the Place, commemorating the entrance into the Salt Lake Valley and the Promised Land.

The park is located off of highway 186 at the mouth of Emigration Canyon in the eastern part of Salt Lake City. Within the city are many other sites of historical interest for those concerned with the Mormon migration, and they also deserve the attention of modern travelers.

Soda Springs, Idaho

This was the site of the famous Steamboat Springs and geyser that many emigrants wrote about. Unfortunately, today it is covered by the reservoir and cannot be viewed. Just north of the city of Soda Springs is the famous Hooper Springs. It is located in a city park. One can drink the water there as emigrants did, but there is no display concerning it. Within the heart of the city is a man-controlled geyser, which is of special interest to the children, and the cone is similar to those the emigrants would have seen and that were painted by Wilkins.

Fort Hall, Idaho

The site of the actual fort is on the Fort Hall Indian Reservation and is identified only by a marker. However, a reproduction of the fort has been built and can be visited. In it are displays from the fur-trapping era and the emigrant period.

The reproduction of Fort Hall can be found at Ross Park and Zoo south of the city of Pocatello off I-15. The children will enjoy roaming about both the fort and zoo.

City of Rocks and Steeple Rock, Almo, Idaho

Through this natural circular valley passed the emigrants who use the Fort Hall and Hudspeth Cutoff. At the southern end of the valley is the famous Steeple Rock or Twin Sisters which also marked the junction of the California Trail with the Salt Lake Road. While there is no display in the area the remnants of the trail can still be seen cutting through the valley. There are also small picnic areas one in the southern section by Steeple Rock and another in the western section.

City of Rocks is located near Almo, Idaho off highway 77.

Northeastern Nevada Museum, Nevada

The area around Elko was a camping area for the westward emigrants. A few miles to the south the Hastings Cutoff joined the main California Trail. The museum primarily focuses on the Indian, pioneer, and mining period of this region.

It is located on business I-80 by the city park in Elko, Nevada.

Fort Churchill State Historic Monument, Nevada

This fort was built in 1860 on the alternate river route of the Carson Trail at the end of the period considered in this book. It was constructed to protect the emigrants and pioneers in the Carson River Valley. The fort was abandoned in 1869 and sold by 1870. There is a visitor center and interpretive displays related to its military role in the area. The fort is in ruins but one can imagine what it might have been like by walking around the area. Remnants of the trail are still visible in the area. Camping, picnicking, and hiking are available on the grounds.

The fort is located about ten miles south of Silver Springs off of U.S. Highway 95 on CR 2B, U.S. alternative route 50.

Mormon Station Historic State Monument, Nevada

Here is a replica of the Mormon Station, which was constructed in 1850. It includes a stockade and trading post. Many emigrants stopped here on the Carson route. They were able to rest briefly and obtain needed supplies before their hard pull over the Sierra Nevada. Mormon Station was shortly renamed Genoa by Orson Hyde, an early emigrant, because the area reminded him of the mountains behind Genoa, Italy.

The station is lcoated on SR 57 off I-395 in Genoa, Nevada.

Donner Memorial State Park, California

Here is the monument and museum concerning that fateful winter of 1846 for the Donner party on the Truckee route. They spent that winter in this vicinity. As noted earlier in the history section of this volume, many members of the party were forced into cannibalism in order to survive that dreadful winter. In addition to the visitor center there are facilities for camping, hiking, fishing, and swimming.

The park is located off I-80 on U.S. Highway 10 near Truckee, California.

Lessen Volcanic National Park, California

Within this park are remnants of the Nobles's Road. This was the cutoff that was opened in 1852. Today you can hike along part of that trail.

Information can be obtained at the visitor centers at the entrances to the park. The park is located on California Highway 89 in northern California. It is about fifty miles east of Redding.

Sutter's Fort, California

This is the site of Sutter's "New Helvetia," the goal of most of the early emigrants and the end of the California Trail. Today Sutter's Fort has been reconstructed to appear as it did just before the gold rush. The restored central adobe building is the only remaining original structure, the rest having been reconstructed. There are a variety of displays concerning its role in the early history of California. Unfortunately for Sutter when gold was discovered it did not bring him wealth as he thought it might have, but instead it resulted in the destruction of his empire.

The fort is located on Twentieth and L Street in Sacramento. Within Sacramento are other points of historical interest which travelers may want to look up.

Marshall Gold Discovery State Historic Park, California

Here is the site of the gold discovery made by Marshall in 1848. A museum and a replica of the mill that was being constructed when the gold was discovered are on the grounds. Marshall is buried in the park. Within the town are other buildings from the gold rush era.

The park is located on California Highway 49 in the town of Coloma, California.

Placerville, California—Historic District

This is one of the many early gold rush towns that developed in 1848-49. It was originally known as "Dry Diggings" but soon became known as "Hangtown" because it was the first gold rush town to use hanging as the method of dealing with lawbreakers. This was the goal of Betsey and Ike of the song in the beginning of the book. Today there are a number of buildings that date from the gold rush era. There are also a number of events related to its early history that would be of interest to the traveler. One is the annual wagon train celebration held in June. It starts out at Lake Tahoe and follows U.S. Highway 50, which closely approximates the Johnson's Cutoff of the Carson route into Placerville. (An early view of "Hangtown" is included in the pictorial section.)

Placerville is located at the intersection of U.S. 50 and California Highway 49.

For any traveler primarily interested in the gold rush era California Highway 49 from Mariposa in the south to Sierraville in the north traverses the area frequently called the "Mother Load." Most of the small towns are associated with the gold rush and have buildings from that period. Many have small museums or sites of interest. This area was the goal and "El Dorado" that the forty-niners sought.

In addition to the places mentioned above, there are numerous highway historical markers and displays along the way or in the rest areas that are not included in this book that can provide the modern "emigrant" with information about the trail to California. They usually do not require more than a few minutes stop at each one, but they do add to one's understanding of the trek to California and should be examined.

Additional Reading

There are a variety of books available on the overland or emigrant trails. Every year new books both large and small are coming out. Because the main California Trail was the same as the Oregon Trail for more than the first half, it gives us a place to begin our investigation into the publications available for your use as a modern emigrant or argonaut along the California Trail.

For the part of the California Trail that coincided with the Oregon Trail there are two very fine books written by Gregory Franzwa. The two books actually supplement each other.

The first is *The Oregon Trail Revisited* and the second is *Maps of the Oregon Trail*. The first takes the reader mile by mile and turn by turn along the modern highways and farm roads that most closely follow the twists and turns of the old emigrant trail. Along with this milepost approach to the trail, there are comments from various emigrants who had taken it themselves. When there are places where the modern traveler might not be able to venture in a passenger car these places are noted. The important historic sites along the way are also mentioned and their significance is explained. While the book does not include all the routes from the jumping-off places, the modern traveler can use this as a guide from Independence, Missouri, and drive along most of the trail all the way past Fort Hall to the Raft River where the California Trail turns off.

The second of his books is perhaps even better for the traveler who reads maps well and can visualize the trip. Again the emphasis is on the main Oregon Trail from Independence, Missouri, so the book is primarily useful for the same section of the California Trail as mentioned above. The trail shows up as a thin red line on his maps. Most of the maps are drawn having a scale of one-half inch to a mile and include not only the main roads but also the farm roads. The book also refers to many of the very important cutoffs, which were not included in his first book. Additionally, his maps are constantly being updated for the most recent discoveries concerning the trail. The location of large segments of visible trail ruts are also located on the maps as are the related historic sites. Therefore, they are much easier for the present-day traveler to find and see.

Another related book is *Historic Sites along the Oregon Trail* by Aubrey Haines. It contains the specific locations of 394 sites of which 318 also apply to the California Trail section. These same sites are also located in Franzwa's book of maps. They include things such as major forts, crossings, locations of graves, landmarks, and even prominent camping grounds with emigrant comments about each place.

Using these three books, locating and traveling the first part of the California Trail, is easy and enjoyable.

For a historic overview of the development of the trail and the various jumping-off places mentioned earlier in the book there is Merrill Mattes's book *The Great Platte River Road*. It covers the trails from their various points of origin through the Platte River Valley to Fort Laramie. The book includes a wealth of information and the trail is vividly described by the extensive use of primary source materials.

Another book, which also gives the reader a broad overview of the emigrant experience, is John Unruh's *The Plains Across*. Unlike the other books already mentioned it does not take the reader mile by mile along the trail, but instead discusses the development of the California and Oregon trails over time. It examines the forces that impacted on the trails and their interrelationships. Various topics, such as, improvements in the trail, Indians, Mormons, trading posts, the government, emigrant motivations and opinions, are all discussed. This approach coupled with the above book gives the modern traveler an excellent perspective of the trail experienced by the emigrants.

Perhaps the best book for describing the historical development of the California Trail is George Stewart's *The California Trail: An Epic with Many Heroes*. This book has just been reprinted and is now available. It covers the development of the trail starting with the Bartleson-Bidwell party in 1841. From that period until the gold rush era it has a chapter for each year. It mentions the wagon companies for each year and the major ones for the years when travel was heavy. After the gold rush in 1849 the major routes were developed and the trail was established. Stewart spends less time on the developments during the 1850s. The book includes many small maps showing the locations of the trails and the various cutoffs with the years of their development. It gives one a good overview of the whole developmental period.

For locating the California Trail where Franzwa's books left off there are a few suggested books. One of the most recently published works is *Emigrant Trails West* by Devere and Helene Helfrich and Thomas Hunt. It is *A Guide to Trail Markers Placed by Trails West, Inc. Along the California, Applegate, Lassen, and Nobles's Emigrant Trails in Idaho, Nevada, and California*. It includes maps of the trail drawn with a scale of four miles to an inch, the specific locations of 201 trail markers, and excerpts from diaries concerning each of the locations. Using the maps it takes the reader from marker to marker starting at the Raft River where the main California Trail leaves the Oregon Trail. It then continues down the main route of the California Trail to where the Applegate Trail turns off, and the Lassen Trail begins. *Emigrant Trails West* also shows where the Nobles's route cuts off from both the Lassen and Applegate trails and follows the California Trail. However, it must be noted that this book does not include the sections for the Truckee and Carson routes that were developed before 1848 nor the Hastings Cutoff.

There is a smaller publication by the Nevada Historical Society called *The Overland Emigrant Trail to California*. It is *A Guide to Trail Markers Placed in Western Nevada and the Sierra Nevada Mountains in California*, which is helpful for the Truckee and Carson trails. The Historical Society has placed fifty-eight markers starting at the point where the Applegate-Lassen trails branch off and then following the trail down the Humboldt to the split in the Carson and Truckee trails. It then follows both up the mountains to the divide, but it unfortunately goes no further. Its two main maps are drawn at a scale of nine miles to an inch and five miles to an inch, which are fairly small. They do include directions to the markers and a description of the markers. However, they do not include excerpts from emigrant diaries for each location.

A third book unfortunately is no longer available. It was produced by the Bureau of Land Management in Idaho, Department of the Interior. It was called *Emigrant Trails in Southeastern Idaho*, and it includes the main trail to Fort Hall and then down the Raft River, the Hudspeth Cutoff, and part of the Salt Lake Cutoff. If you can get a copy it is very good, having both maps and emigrant comments about the areas.

In addition to the scholarly approach to the study of the California Trail there are a number of narratives and diaries of emigrants along the trail. Bruff traveled the trail in 1849. His diary and writings are the source of many of the drawings in the pictorial section of this volume. Unfortunately, his journal published as *Gold Rush: Journals, Drawings, and Other Papers* can be found only in libraries. The work published in 1949 was edited by George Read and Ruth Gaines and is excellent. Bruff was the captain of the company and he noted almost "everything." His route took him to Fort Hall and down over the Lassen or "Greenhorn" route to California. Additonal information about Bruff is included in the pictorial section.

One of the journals that has recently been published is *The California Gold Rush Overland Diary of Bryon McKinstry*. This was published in 1975 and is still available. It includes both the diary of Bryon McKinstry and also comments made by his grandson Bruce McKinstry as he tried to relocate and retrace the specific route taken to California by his grandfather. McKinstry went to California by way of the Sublette Cutoff, Fort Hall, and the Carson route. It should also be noted that McKinstry was also in the company that pioneered the route on the northern side of the North Platte west of Fort Laramie and rejoined the main trail west of Deer Creek where many of the other emigrants started crossing over. The book is interesting both for its historical narrative and for the experience of one trying to locate specific sites along the California Trail.

Another of the interesting and recently published books is *Overland to California with the Pioneer Line: The Gold Rush Diary of Bernard J. Reid* edited by Mary Gordon. The Pioneer Line was the first commercial venture to bring emigrants and gold seekers to California. The venture was mentioned a number of times by James Wilkins whose drawings are included in the pictorial section. The book includes not only the diary, but also additional comments made later in life by Bernard Reid. Gordon also included many comments from the diaries of other members of the train, and thus affords the reader a variety of perspectives on this first commercial and problem-filled venture.

These are but a few of the many works that a student of the trail would enjoy. There is a new series called *Covered Wagon Women: Diaries and Letters from the Western Trails 1840-1890* by Arthur H. Clark Publishers.

As of this date, five volumes are available for the earliest years. Other publishers such as Ye Galleon Press offers reprints of earlier published works on a limited scale. They have a number of fine reprints available for order. One older book which is almost considered a classic, is Irene Paden's *The Wake of the Prairie Schooner* has recently been republished. She traveled the old trails during the 1930s and describes both her experiences and the trail as they existed then.

Additionally, the journals of the various state and local historical societies are another fine source for diaries and should not be overlooked. The publication of the Oregon-California Trails Association *The Overland Journal* published quarterly is another excellent source of material. It even includes information about the present condition of the trail and efforts aimed at its preservation. There are also many books available that focus in on specific topics such as the Donner party, John Sutter, or the gold rush. One other area, which must be mentioned, is the bibliographies of all the books mentioned. They are full of outstanding source materials, which you may find of interest.

Happy Reading !   Happy Traveling!

Bibliography

Books, Booklets, and Articles

Driggs, Howard R. *Westward America*. New York: J.B. Lippincott, 1942.

Estergreen, M. Morgan. *Kit Carson: A Portrait in Courage*. Norman: University of Oklahoma Press, 1962.

Franzwa, Gregory. *Maps of the Oregon Trail*. Gerald, Mo.: Patrice Press, 1982.

Franzwa, Gregory. *The Oregon Trail Revisited*. Gerald, Mo.: Patrice Press, 1972.

Froncek, Thomas. "Winterkill, 1846. The Tragic Journey of the Donner Party." *American Heritage*. December 1976, Vol. XXVIII, No. 1 pp. 29-42.

Ghent, W.J. *The Road to Oregon, A Chronicle of the Great Emigrant Trail*. New York: Tudor, 1934.

Gilbert, William, and others. *The Trail Blazers*. New York: Time/Life Books, 1973.

Haines, Aubrey. *Historic Sites along the Oregon Trail*. Gerald, Mo.: Patrice Press, 1981.

Harris, Earl R. *Courthouse and Jail Rocks*. Nebraska State Historical Society, 1962.

Helfrich, Devere and Helene, and Thomas Hunt. *Emigrant Trails West*. Klamath Falls, Oreg.: Craft Printers, Trails West, Inc. 1984.

Hill, William E. *Along the Oregon Trail, Yesterday and Today*. Caldwell, Idaho: The Caxton Printers, Ltd., 1986.

Horn, Houston. *The Pioneers*. New York: Time/Life Books, 1974.

Jackson, Clarance S. *Picture Maker of the Old West, William H. Jackson*. New York: Bonanza Books, Inc., 1947.

Jackson, Donald Dale. *Gold Dust*. New York: Alfred A. Knopf, Inc., 1980.

Jackson, Joseph Henry, ed. *Gold Rush Album*. New York: Bonanza Books, 1949.

Jackson, William Henry. *Time Exposure*. New York: G.P. Putnam's Sons, 1940.

Johnson, Paul C. *Pictorial History of California*. New York: Bonanza Books, 1970.

Lavender, David. *California: A Bicentennial History*. New York: W.W. Norton & Company, Inc., 1976.

———. *The American Heritage History of the Great West*. New York: Bonanza Books, 1982.

Laxalt, Robert, and others. *Trails West*. Washington, D.C.: National Georaphic Society, 1979.

Lewis, Oscar. *Sutter's Fort: Gateway to the Gold Fields*. Englewood Cliffs, N.J.: Prentice Hall, Inc., 1966.

Mattes, Merrill J. *Chimney Rock Nebraska*. Nebraska State Historical Society, 1978.

———. *The Great Platte River Road*. Nebraska State Historical Society, 1969.

———. *Scotts Bluff*. Washington, D.C.: National Park Service, 1976.

———. "The Council Bluffs Road: the Northern Branch of the Great Platte River Road," *Nebraska History*, Vol. 65 (1984), pp. 179-194.

Mokler, Alfred James. *Fort Caspar*. Casper, Wyo.: The Prairie Publishing Co., 1939. Reprint: Mountain States Lithographing Co., 1982.

Moody, Ralph. *The Old Trails West*. N.Y.: T.Y. Crowell Co., 1963.

Paden, Irene D. *The Wake of the Prairie Schooner*. New York: The Macmillan Company, 1947.

Place, Marian T. *Westward on the Oregon Trail*. New York: American Heritage Publishing Co., Inc., 1962.

Ross, Marvin C. *The West of Alfred J. Miller*. Norman: University of Oklahoma Press, 1968.

Schlissel, Lillian. *Women's Diaries of the Westward Journey*. New York: Schocken Books, 1982.

Stewart, George R. *The California Trail: An Epic with Many Heroes*. New York: McGraw-Hill Book Co., Inc., 1962.

Troner, Ellen Lloyd, ed. *California, a Chronology and Documentary Handbook*. Dobbs Ferry, N.Y.: Oceana Publications, Inc., 1972.

Unruh, John. *The Plains Across, the Overland Emigrants and the Trans-Mississippi West, 1940-60*. Chicago: University of Illinois Press, 1979.

Wagner, Henry R. *The Plains and the Rockies: A Bibliography of Original Narratives of Travel and Adventure 1800-1865*. Columbus: Long's College Book, Co., 1953.

Wheat, Carl I. *Mapping the Trans-Mississippi West*. Vol. III. San Francisco: Institute of Historical Cartography, 1957.

———. *Emigrant Trails of Southeastern Idaho*. Bureau of Land Management, U.S. Department of Interior, Idaho, 1979.

———. "The Raft River in Idaho History." *Pacific Northwest Quarterly*. July 1941, Vol. 32, pp. 289-305.

———. *Story of the Great American West*. Pleasantville, N.Y.: The Reader's Digest Association, Inc., 1977.

———. *Oregon Trail, National Historic Trail, Comprehensive Management and Use Plan*. Appendix II & III. National Park Service, August 1981.

———. *The Overland Emigrant Trail to California*. Nevada Historical Society.

Diaries, Journals, and Guidebooks

Applegate, Jesse. "A Day with the Cow Column in 1843." *Oregon Historical Quarterly*. Vol. I, December 1900, pp. 371-383.

Baker, William. *Diary of William B. Baker—California 1852*. Ventura Historical Museum.

Borthwick, J.D. *Three Years in California*. William Blackwood and Sons, 1857.

Bruff, J. Goldsborough. *Gold Rush: Journals, Drawings, and Other Papers*. Edited by Georgia Willis Read and Ruth Gaines. New York: Columbia Press, 1949.

Bryant, Edwin. *What I Saw in California*. New York: D. Appleton and Co., 1849.

Bryarly, Wakeman and Vincent Geiger. *Trail to California. The Overland Journal of Vincent Geiger and Wakeman Bryarly*. Edited by David Potter. New Haven: Yale University Press, 1945.

Burnett, Peter H. "Recollections and Opinions of an Old Pioneer." *Oregon Historical Quarterly*. Vol. V, 1904, pp. 64-99.

Casler, Mel. *A Journal Giving the Incidents of a Journey to California in the Summer of 1859, by the Overland Route.* Fairfield, Wash.: Ye Galleon Press, 1969.

Child, Andrew. *Overland Route to California.* Milwaukee: Daily Sentinel Steam Power Press, 1852.

Clayton, William. *The Latter-Day Saints' Emigrants' Guide.* St. Louis: Champers & Knapp, 1848. Reprint: Fairfield, Wash.: Ye Galleon Press, 1981.

Clyman, James. *Journal of a Mountain Man.* Edited by Linda M. Hasselstrom. Missoula: Mountain Press Publishing Co., 1984.

Dundass, Samuel Rutherford and George Keller. *The Journals of Samuel Rutherford Dundass & George Keller. Crossing the Plains to California in 1849-1850.* Fairfield, Wash.: Ye Galleon Press, 1983.

Farnham, Elijah Bryan. "From Ohio to California: the Gold Rush Journal of — ——, edited by Merrill J. Mattes, *Indiana Magazine of History*, XLVI (1950), pp. 297-318, 403-420.

Frémont, John Charles. *The Expeditions of J.C. Fremont.* 1 and 2, maps. Edited by Donald Jackson and Mary Lee Spence. Urbana: University of Illinois Press, 1970.

Gordon, Mary. ed. *Overland to California with the Pioneer Line: The Gold Rush Diary of Bernard J. Reid.* Stanford: Standord University Press, 1983.

Hale, Israel. "Diary of Trip to California." *Society of California Pioneers Quarterly.* Vol. 2, 1925, pp. 61-130.

Hastings, Lansford. *The Emigrants' Guide to Oregon and California.* 1845. Reprint Princeton: Princeton University Press, 1932.

Holmes, Kenneth L. ed. *Covered Wagon Women: Diaries and Letters from the Western Trails 1840-1890.* Glendale, Calif: Arthur H. Clark. Vol. I & II, 1983.

Horn, Hosea. *Horn's Overland Guide.* New York: J.H. Colton, 1853.

Hulin, Lester. *Day Book or Journal of Lester Hulin 1847.* Eugene, Oreg.: Lane County Historical Society, 1959.

Huston, Henry Clay. *Diaries of Henry Clay Huston, 1856-1860.* Eugene, Oreg.: Lane County Historical Society, 1960.

Ingalls, Eleazar Stillman. *Journal of a Trip to California by Overland Route Across the Plains in 1850-1.* Fairfield, Wash.: Ye Galleon Press, 1979.

Ingersoll, Chester. *Overland to California in 1847.* Fairfield, Wash.: Ye Galleon Press, 1970.

Kerns, John T. "Journal of Crossing the Plains to Oregon in 1852." *Transactions,* O.P.A., 1914, pp. 148-193.

Leinhard, Heinrich. *From St. Louis to Sutter's Fort, 1846.* Edited by Erwin & Elizabeth Gudde. Norman: University of Oklahoma Press, 1961.

McKinstry, Bryon N. *The California Gold Rush Overland Diary of Bryon N. McKinstry.* Edited by Bruce L. McKinstry. Glendale, Calif.: The Arthur H. Clark Co., 1975.

Marcy, Randolph B. *The Prairie Traveler, A Handbook for Overland Expeditions.* New York: Harper & Bros., 1859.

Paden, Irene. "The Ira J. Willis Guide to the Gold Mines." *California Historical Society Quarterly,* XXXII. 1953, pp. 193-207.

Page, Elizabeth. *Wagons West.* New York: Farra & Rinehart, Inc., 1930. (Diary & Letters of Henry Page, 1849.)

Parkman, Francis, Jr. *The California and Oregon Trail.* New York: William L. Allison Co., 18— [1849].

Piercy, Frederick. *Route from Liverpool to Great Salt Lake Valley.* Edited by Fawn M. Brodie. Cambridge: The Belknap Press of Harvard University Press, 1962.

Pleasants, William. *Twice across the Plains—1849 & 1856.* Fairfield, Wash.: Ye Galleon Press, 1981.

Reading P.B. "Journal of Pierson Barton Reading." *Society of California Pioneers, Quarterly.* Vol. 6, 1930, pp. 148-198.

Shively, J.M. *Route and Distances to Oregon and California.* Washington: W. Greer, Printer, 1846.

Smith, C.W. *Journal of a Trip to California—Across the Continent from Weston, Missouri to Weber Creek, California in the Summer of 1850.* Edited by R.W.G. Vail. Fairfield, Wash.: Ye Galleon Press, 1974.

Snyder, Jacob R. "The Diary of Jacob R. Snyder—1845." *Society of California Pioneers, Quarterly.* 1931, Vol. 8, pp. 224-260.

Stansbury, Howard. *An Expedition to the Valley of the Great Salt Lake.* Philadelphia: Lippincott, Grambo, and Co., 1852.

Street, Frank. *Concise Description of the Overland Route.* Cincinnati: R.F. Edwards & Co., 1851.

Ware, Joseph. *The Emigrants' Guide to California.* St. Louis: J. Halsall, 1849.

Wilkins, James F. *An Artist on the Overland Trail, The Diary of James F. Wilkins, 1849.* Edited by John F. McDermott. San Marino: The Huntington Library, 1968.

Woodworth, James. *Diary of James Woodworth across the Plains to California in 1853.* Eugene, Oreg.: Lane County Historical Society, 1972.

Pamphlets

"Chimney Rock," National Park Service, Washington, D.C., 1974.

"The Donner Party," Donner Memorial State Park, Department of Parks & Recreation, Sacramento, 1977.

"Fort Bridger," Wyoming Recreation Department, State Archives & Historical Department.

"Fort Caspar Museum," Casper, Wyo.

"Fort Churchill," Nevada Division of State Parks, *Nevada Magazine.*

"Fort Kearny," Nebraska State Historical Society. Ed. Leaflet No. 7.

"Fort Laramie," National Park Service, Washington, D.C.

"Hollenberg Pony Express Station," Kansas State Historical Society, Topeka, Kans.

"Marshall Gold Discovery State Historic Park," Department of Parks & Recreation, Sacramento, Calif.

"Mormon Station," Nevada Division of State Parks, *Nevada Magazine,* 1979.

"The Oregon Trail," National Park Service, Washington, D.C.

"The Oregon Trail," Nebraska Game and Parks Commission.

"Rock Creek Station," Nebraska Game and Parks Commission.

"Route of the Oregon Trail in Idaho," Idaho Historical Society Bicentennial Commission and the Idaho Transportation Department, 1974.

"Salt Lake Sites," Salt Lake Convention & Visitors Bureau, Salt Lake City, Utah.

"Scotts Bluff," National Park Service, Washington, D.C., 1978.

"Self-Guided Tour of Fort Leavenworth the Gateway to the West," Fort Leavenworth Historical Society, Ft. Leavenworth, Kans., 1982.

"Weston, Queen of the Steamboat Days, Old Homes Tour," The Weston Historical Museum, 1972.

Index

Adams-Onis Treaty, 8
Alcove Spring, 14, 76, 77
Alexander Von Humboldt, 7
Allen & Turner. *See* Pioneer Line
Almo, ID, 176, 177
Almo Creek Massacre, 10
Alvarado, Juan B., 9, 11
American River, 8, 10, 15
Ampitheatre, 129
Antelope Spring, 20
Apollo, 5, 22
Applegate, Jesse, 14
Applegate Trail, 14, 16, 19, 156, 180
Ash Hollow, 86, 174
Aspenwall, Wills, 4

Baker, William, 40
Baker-Davis Cutoff/Road, 11, 19, 136
Bartleson-Bidwell party. *See* Bidwell
Battle Mountain, 155
Beach, John, 5
Bear Flag Revolt, 9, 13, 14
Bear, Chief Conquering, 19
Bear River, 141, 142, 145
Bear Mountains, 142, 143
Beckwourth, Jim, 18, 169
Beckwourth Pass, 18, 169
Bennington, ID, 143
Bessemer Bend, 98
Bidwell, John & party, 10, 11, 15, 17, 19
Big Blue River, 76
Big Hill, 141
Big Sandy, 12
Big Trees Route, 19
Bishops Creek, 9
Black Rock Desert, 6, 40, 158, 162
Black's Fork, 11
Bonneville, Benjamin, 12
Borthwick, J.D., 5
Brady Cabin, 70
Brannan, Samuel, 14, 15
Bridgeport, NE, 175
Bridger, Jim, 11, 14, 17, 33, 127, 173
Bridger Butte, 126, 128
Brigham City, 20
Bruff, J. Goldsborough, 6, 17, 23, 32, 34, 40, 60-61, 104, 106, 118, 137, 138, 139, 140, 146, 147, 148, 150, 151, 152, 155, 156-157, 158, 159, 160, 161, 171, 180
Brule, NE, 84, 85, 174
Bryant, Edwin, 14, 23, 42, 77
Bryarly, Wakeman, 40, 42-49, 145
buffalo chips, 7
Burnett, Peter, 17, 18
Burnt Ranch, 2, 20
Butterfield Stage Line, 20

Calder Creek, 12
California, 7
California Hill, 84, 85
California Revolt. *See* Bear Flag Revolt
Campbell, Robert, 9
Cape Horn, 3, 4, 5
Carson, Kit, 9, 11, 12, 13, 55, 57
Carson Canyon, 165
Carson River, 16, 40, 53, 57, 58, 59, 177
Carson Route, 2, 16, 19, 20, 34, 36, 164, 178, 180
Carson Sink, 6, 16, 57
Case Ferry, 136
Casper, WY, 2, 98, 176
Castro, Jose, 9
Cathedral Rock. *See* Church Butte
Cave Spring, 173
Central America, 5
Central Overland California and Pike's Peak Express, 20
Charges River, 23
Child, Andrew, 33
Chiles, Joseph, 11, 12, 15, 16, 51
Chimney Rock, 88, 89, 174, 175
cholera, 5, 18
Church Butte, 124, 125
City of Rocks, 12, 16, 20, 36, 149, 150, 151, 152, 176, 177
Clark, George, 21, 23
Clayton, William, 33, 34, 35
Clyman, James, 14, 16
Cogswell, Mores, 6
Collins, Lt. Caspar, 20
Coloma, CA, 167, 178
Colton, Walter, 15
Cokeville, ID, 142
Compromise of 1850, 18
costs, 3, 4
Council Bluffs, 2, 15, 75
Council Bluffs Road, 2, 6. *See also* Mormon Trail
Court House Rock, 87, 174, 175

Death Valley, 3
death, 3, 5, 51-52, 56, 66, 156
Deep Creek Cutoff, 16. *See also* Salt Lake Road/Cutoff
Deer Creek, 63, 97, 98
DeSmet, Father Pierre-Jean, 8, 11
Devil's Gate, 105, 106, 107, 176
Devil's Slide, 133
Digger Indians, 13
Dingle Station, ID, 141
disease, 5
Donner Creek, 15
Donner, George & party, 4, 10, 14, 15, 23, 33, 76, 133, 134, 163
Donner Lake, 13, 15
Donner Pass, 13, 15

Donner Pass State Park, 163, 177
Dry Sandy, 64, 121
Dry Sandy Crossing, 120, 121, 137
dust, 64
Dry Diggings. *See* Placerville

Echo Canyon, 129, 130, 131, 132
elephant, 40
Elizabeth, 6
Elko, NV, 177
Emigration Canyon, 134, 176

Fairbury, NE, 174
ferries, 4, 75
Ferris, Warren, 9
fire, 7
First Fort Laramie Treaty. *See* Treaty of Horse Creek
Fitzpatrick, Tom, 8, 11
Fly Canyon, 160
Florence, NE, 75
Fontenelle Bluffs, 140
Fort Boise, 12
Fort Bridger, 2, 11, 20, 23, 33, 34, 121, 122, 124, 126, 127, 128, 129, 176
Fort Caspar, 99, 175
Fort Childs, 16. *See also* Fort Kearny
Fort Churchill, 20, 164, 177
Fort Hall, 2, 9, 14, 16, 17, 20, 33, 34, 141, 146, 147, 176
Fort John, 10, 92. *See also* Fort Laramie
Fort Hall Indian reservation, 176
Fort Kearny, 2, 4, 80, 82-83, 174
Fort Kearny, South Pass, Honey Lake Wagon Road, 20
Fort Laramie, 4, 92, 93, 95, 175
Fort Leavenworth, 2, 8, 72-73, 173
Fort Ross, 10
Fort Vancouver, 10
Fort William, 9, 10. *See also* Fort Laramie
Forty-Mile Desert, 1, 6, 13, 16, 43-46, 56-59, 162
Franzwa, Gregory, 179, 180
Frémont, John Charles, 11, 12, 13, 17, 43
Frémont's Castle, 159
Fugitive Slave Act, 18

Gaines, Read and Ruth, 180
Gateway Arch, 172
Genoa, NV, 177
Gila River, 2
Gillespie, Lt. Archibald, 138
Goose Creek, 9
Goose Lake, 17
Gordon, Mary, 181
Grattan, Lt. John, 19
graves. *See* death
Great Eastern, 130
Great Migration, 12

Great Salt Lake Desert, 11, 15
Grecian, 5, 6
Green River, 19, 122, 123, 136, 138, 140
Greenhorn Cutoff, 18, 180
Greenwood, Caleb, 12, 33
Greenwood Cutoff, 2, 12, 13, 17. *See also* Sublette Cutoff
Greenwood, John, 13
Greyhound, 5
guidebooks, 3, 33-39
Guinard, Louis, 20

Haines, Aubrey, 179
Hangtown. *See* Placerville
Ham's Fork, 6, 60, 124
Harris, Black, 33
Harrison Pass, 11
Harvey, Charles, 5, 6
Hastings, Lansford, 13, 23, 33, 36, 170
Hastings Cutoff, 14, 15, 23, 33, 34, 173, 177
Hayden Survey, 60
Haystack Butte, 137
Helfrich, Devere and Helene, 180
Henry Lee, 5
Hensley, Samuel, 16, 34, 154
Hershey, NE, 84
Hickok-McCanles shooting, 174
Hidalgo y Costilla, Miguel, 8
Hitchock, Isaac "Old Man," 12
Hollenberg Ranch, 78, 173
Hope Valley, 16
Hooper, Charles, 11, 15
Hooper Spring, 144, 176
Horn, Hosea, 33, 36-39
Hot Spring Valley, 36
Hudson Bay Company, 9, 12
Hudson River, 148
Hudspeth, Benoni, 17
Hudspeth Cutoff, 2, 36, 176, 180
Humboldt River, 2, 9, 23, 33, 40, 42, 43, 44, 55
Humboldt Sink, 2, 6, 13, 16, 40, 42, 43, 57
Hunt, Thomas, 180
Huntington Library, 40, 61
Huston, Henry, 6
Hyde, Orson, 177

Ide, William, 14
Independence, 7
Independence, MO, 2, 8, 10, 11, 23, 69, 70, 172
Independence Crossing, 76
Independence Rock, 8, 100, 101, 102, 103, 104, 105, 176
Independence Square, 8, 69
Indians, 13, 19, 20, 66, 80, 81, 99, 139, 174
Ingalls, Eleazar, 40, 55-59
Ingersoll, Chester, 145
Isthmus of Panama, 3, 4, 5, 23

Jackson, Andrew, 9
Jackson, Donald, 5
Jackson, William H., 60-61, 65, 66, 68, 75, 76, 80, 82, 89, 91, 93, 99, 101, 102, 103, 107, 110, 111, 115, 121, 125, 126, 127, 129, 130, 131, 134, 135, 147, 174
Jail Rock. *See* Court House Rock
Jefferson National Expansion Memorial, 172
Jefferson, Thomas H., 23
John A. Sutter, 5
Johnson's Cutoff, 19, 178
Jones, Commodore, 11
Julesburg, CO, 85
Julesburg Crossing. *See* Upper California Crossing

Kainsville, 2, 75. *See also* Council Bluffs
Keller, George, 6
Kelsey, Nancy and Ann, 11
Kerns, John, 75
Keyes, Sarah, 14, 76
Kimball, Hazen, 16
Kinney Cutoff, 11, 19
Kinney, Sam, 13

Lake Tahoe, 77, 178
Lander, Frederick, 20
Lander Road, 2, 20
Laramie Peak, 10, 95
Larkin, Consul, 13
Lassen Meadows, 16, 32
Lassen, Peter, 12, 16, 17
Lassen Route, 2, 16, 17, 18, 20, 21, 32, 158, 180
Lee Missions, 10
Lodgepole Creek, 84
Lombard Ferry, 122, 123
Loup River, 80
Lower California Crossing, 84, 85

Marsh, John, 9, 10
Marcy, Randolph, 4, 43
Marshall, James, 15, 20, 21, 167, 170, 177
Mary's River, 2, 12, 36, 40, 40-41, 53, 155, *See also* Humboldt River
Massacre Rock, 148
Mattes, Merrill, 40, 179
McCanles, David, 79, 174
McCoy, John C., 9
McDermott, John, 60
McGee, Milton, 17
McKinstry, George, 5, 14, 77, 180-181
McLoughlin, Dr. John, 170
Meek, Joe, 11
Mexican War. *See* Bear Flag Revolt
Miller, Alfred J., 9, 107, 169
Miller, Ellen Independence, 13

Mitchell Pass, 18, 91, 175
Monterey, 11
Montgomery, Captain John, 14
Montpelier, ID, 142
Moore, Joseph, 10
Mormon ferries, 75, 175
Mormon Station, 18, 164
Mormon Trail, 2, 15, 129
Mormons, 2, 14, 15, 17, 34, 65, 173
mules, 3, 19
Murphy, Elizabeth Yuba, 13
Myers, John, 17
Myers Cutoff. *See* Hudspeth Cutoff

National Park Service, 1
Nebraska City, 2, 60
Nevada Historical Society, 1
New Helvetia, 10, 166, 177
New York City, 3, 5, 23
Newberry Library, 36, 40
Nobles, William, 19
Nobles' Road, 19, 177, 180
North Platte River, 98
Northeastern Nevada Museum, 177
Northern Light, 5

Ogden, Peter S., 12
Old Fort Kearny, 2, 16, 74
Old Halter and Flick Ranch, 117
Old Man, 107
Old Spanish Trail, 2, 60
Omaha, NE, 75, 173
Oregon-California Trails Association, 1, 62, 66, 181
Oregon Trail Museum, 18, 61, 175
Oregon Trail Ruts, 175
oxen, 3, 18, 63

Pacific Creek, 116-117
Pacific Springs, 116-117
Paden, Irene, 181
Palmer, Joel, 145
Panama City, 5, 7
Panama Crossing, 3, 4, 21
Parkman, Francis, 10
Parley Canyon, 135
Pawnee Indian Village, KS, 174
Pawnee Museum, 81, 174
Pawnee village, 80-81
Piercy, Frederick, 90
Pilot Peak, 15
Pinnacle Pass, 152, 153
Pioneer Line, 6, 17, 51
Pioneer Trail State Park, 176
Pioneer Village Museum, 61
Placerville, 16, 18, 19, 68, 168, 178
Platte Bridge Station, 99
Platte River, 2, 4, 16, 82, 173, 179
Plume Rock, 120, 121
Pocatello, Chief, 20
Pocatello, ID, 147, 176
Polk, James K., 13, 14

Pony Express, 11, 20, 78, 79, 173, 174, 175
Preuss, Charles, 11, 23
Pulpit Rock, 132
Pyramid Circle. *See* City of Rocks

Rabbit Hole Spring, 20, 156, 157
Rabbit Spring, 11
Raft River, 2, 12, 15
Ragtown, 18
railroads, 9, 20
Rattlesnake Mountains, 105
Rattlesnake River, 34
Red Buttes, 98
Red Hills, 96
Reed, James & family, 14, 15, 23, 77, 171
Reed, Virginia, 34
Register Cliff, 95, 175
rendezvous, 8, 9
Reno, NV, 13
Rio de Janeiro, 6
Robidoux, Joseph, 8
Robidoux Pass, 18, 175
Rock Creek Station, 63, 79, 174
Rocky Ridge, 114
Rookery, The, 73
Ross Park, 147
Ruby Mountains, 11
Russians, 10

Sacramento, 17, 20, 166
Sacramento River, 10, 32, 34
St. Joe Road, 2
St. Joseph, MO, 8, 10, 11, 13, 173
St. Louis, MO, 172
Salt Lake City/Valley, 16, 35, 134, 135, 176
Salt Lake Cutoff/Road, 16, 17, 35, 36, 176
Salt Lake-Los Angeles Road, 3, 60
San Buenaventura River, 8
San Francisco, 3, 5, 7, 14, 16, 17, 67
San Gabriel Missions, 8
Santa Catarina, 7
Santa Fe Trail, 2, 3, 8
Sarcophagus Rock, 150, 151
Scott, Hiram, 9
Scott, Levi, 14
Scotts Bluff, 95, 175
Scotts Bluff National Monument, NE, 61, 65, 175
scurvy, 6, 50, 81
seasickness, 5
Sebus house, 70
Shasta City, 19
Shawnee Methodist Mission, 173
ships, 7, 67. *See also* specific names
Sierra Nevada, 9, 11, 40, 49, 61, 164, 169
Sidley Peak, 97
Silver Springs, 177
Simpson, Captain, 20
Singular Rock, 161
Slate Creek Cutoff, 11, 66, 136

smallpox, 5
Smith Charles W., 64, 104
Smith, Jedediah, 8
Smoke Creek Desert, 19
Snake River, 9, 15
Soda Spring Cutoff. *See* Hudspeth Cutoff
Soda Springs, 11, 17, 60, 144-145, 176
Sonora, 19
Sonora Pass, 11
Sonora Road, 19
South Pass, 2, 17, 23, 115, 116, 117, 118, 176
South Platte, 84, 85
Split Rock, 108, 176
Stansbury, Howard, 127
Steamboat Spring, 145
Steeple Rock, 3, 6, 38, 152, 154, 176, 177
Stephens, Elisha, 12, 169
Stephen-Townsend-Murphy party, 12
Stewart, George, 180
Stewart, Sir William Drummond, 9
Street, Frank, 4
Stocktown, 19
storms, 5, 6, 65
Sublette, William, 9, 11
Sublette Cutoff, 2, 17, 19, 121, 136, 137
Sublettes Flat, 19, 138
Sutter, John, 10, 15, 170
Sutter's Fort, 10, 166, 177
Sutter's Mill, 21, 167, 170
Sweden, 6
"Sweet Betsey from Pike," 1, 41
Sweet Water Butte, 108
Sweetwater Pass, 105
Sweetwater River, 103, 108-109

Talcahuano, 7
Tappan, William Henry, 147
Taylor, Zachary, 14, 147
Thousand Springs Valley, 39
Three Crossing Stage Station, 110, 111
Three Crossings, 110, 111, 112, 113
Trails West, Inc., 1
Tragedy Springs, 16
Treaty of Guadalupe Hildago, 16
Treaty of Horse Creek, 18
Tribbetts, Bennett, 110
Truckee, 13, 15, 177
Truckee River, 13, 40, 46
Truckee Route, 2, 23, 40, 42, 43, 177, 180
Tyler, John, 12
Twin Mounds, 115
Twin Sisters, 16, 176. *See also* Steeple Rock

Union, 5
Union Pacific Railroad, 60
Unruh, John, 3, 179
Upper California Crossing, 84, 85

Valparaiso, 7
Vasquez, Louis, 11, 76

Wagon Hound Creek Crossing, 96
Walker, Joseph, 9, 12, 33, 169
Walker Pass, 9, 169
Ware, Joseph, 17, 33, 34
Warp, Harold. *See* Pioneer Village Museum
Wasatch Mountains, 14
Washington City and California Mining Association, 17, 61
Weber Canyon, 14, 131, 133
Western Emigration Society, 10
Weston, 2, 50, 70, 71, 72, 172, 174
Westport, 2, 9, 10, 11, 173
Westport Landing, 9, 68
Whitman Mission, 10
Wilkins, James, 3, 4, 10, 34, 40, 56, 60, 70, 72-73, 74, 80-81, 82-83, 84, 86, 87, 88-89, 92, 95, 96, 97, 100, 106, 108-109, 112, 113, 114, 122, 123, 124, 126, 128, 141, 142, 144-145, 149
Willis, Ira, 33, 34, 35, 36
Wind River Mountains, 113, 114, 115, 118, 119
Windlass Hill, 86, 174
Winter Quarters, 75, 173
Woodbury, Lieutenant, 16
Woodworth, James, 6
Wyeth, Nathaniel, 9

Yale University Library, 41, 61
Yellowstone, 60
Yosemite, 35, 169
Young, Brigham, 11, 15, 132, 176
Yreka Road, 19